PTSD and Attachment Theory

2 Books in 1

a Complete Guide

Trauma Overcoming, Recovery, Attachment Style and Emotional Focused Therapy (EFT)

Greg Watson

The information herein is offered for informational purposes solely, and is universal as so. The presentation of the information is without contract or any type of guarantee assurance.

The trademarks that are used are without any consent, and the publication of the trademark is without permission or backing by the trademark owner. All trademarks and brands within this book are for clarifying purposes only and are the owned by the owners themselves, not affiliated with this document.

THE PTSD WORKBOOK

Skills and Techniques to Overcoming Trauma and Start Recovering

Greg Watson

The information herein is offered for informational purposes solely, and is universal as so. The presentation of the information is without contract or any type of guarantee assurance.

The trademarks that are used are without any consent, and the publication of the trademark is without permission or backing by the trademark owner. All trademarks and brands within this book are for clarifying purposes only and are the owned by the owners themselves, not affiliated with this document.

TABLE OF CONTENTS

What do you do at 3am in the morning when you cannot sleep after a tragic event? First, you recognize how the event affects you, and then you allow your brain to process the information and tell you how to react. I wrote this chapter in the morning after the Columbine High School shootings (at my home in Littleton, Colorado) to remind myself of the pain, how humans usually respond, and how to cope with it. Later, I learnt that people find this information useful in other trauma and disaster circumstances.

Survivors, who have undergone trauma in childhood, including a natural disaster, injury, or childhood abuse, frequently fail to recover through puberty and young adulthood. Teenagers and young adults sometimes feel helpless because they don't know how to help their loved ones. It can make a big difference to learn how trauma affects people and what they can do to help their recovery process.

Memory trauma is felt in many respects, including sexual abuse, war, and violence, to name a few. There are also fewer apparent phobias and more irrational fears of certain things, e.g., bananas. Trauma can also occur in the form of intermittent fear, anxiety, and depression. In these cases, the patient often does not know what caused them and cannot remember any trauma. In the latter type, the brain has stopped the original trauma and/or transmitted the symptoms for a number of reasons.

CHAPTER ONE

WHAT IS TRAUMA?

Trauma is often described as small t trauma and large T trauma, or soft and hard trauma. This concept of trauma depends on incidents. This looks from the outside in rather than from the inside out. In my experience, it is not the incident itself, which is crucial in determining what is traumatic, but how the event or incidents is handled and resolved. Trauma is an individual experience, and it is special for us, our situation, our age, and our available resources to respond to and overcome it. Any unresolved or inexperienced experience may contribute to trauma.

The experience could remain unresolved in many ways. If we have ever felt weak or inadequate, and like our survival, it was potentially painful for us to experience anything. We can be deeply hurt, and injured. The word trauma comes from Greek and literally means harm-by something, mentally, sexually, and psychologically, and if we can't treat it, it can result in trauma. When we freeze and cannot unload the freeze response for any reason, it will also cause trauma in our system. The traumatic event can then be caused or replicated before relief is found. When there are no more freeze reactions, and chronic pain is not overcome, a tremendous burden is placed on our body, and our endurance is seriously reduced.

One of the most debilitating and persistent traumas is the recurrent experience of unloving and unwelcome emotions, which often starts in the womb. If a baby feels unloved and unwanted, it can be seen as a real threat to his life and can lead to impoverishment and hopelessness. The unloved wounds go very deep and are mostly inexperienced or frozen just because they are so painful. In order to solve these wounds, the imprint is traced and re-enacted in all kinds of different ways. We still look for resolution, we need resolution.

If the essential need for love is not met, children learn to mistrust and deny all their needs, because unless they are worthy of love, they are not worthy of being loved. Through traumatic experiences as early as our time through the womb, freezing often becomes the conditioned response when we feel threatened by lower resilience later in life. Our life stress level is compromised by unresolved trauma, and we are hyper-vigilant, vulnerable, dissociated, anxious, and depressed, we do everything to sedate our pain.

TRAUMATIC STRESS DISORDER

The term ' trauma' has two meanings in medicine:

> Some of your body has been unexpectedly destroyed by a force that's so strong that it's the body's natural shape, such as your head, skull, and so on.
> Injuries when natural body healing is inadequate to repair the wounds without medical treatment.

At the psychological level, trauma now applies to injure your heart, mind, and will to live, self-confidence, and the world around you, your pride, and your sense of self-assurance. The effect of the traumatic event on your emotions has been so severe that the usual way of life, thought, and feeling is turned downside, so the way you handle stress becomes ineffective in the past. There are many problems in your lifetime, some of which are minor and some of which are large every day, losing your wallet to face the loss of one's wife or family member. Even in most of these cases, it is stressful and can often describe traumatic events, but in technical terms, they are not really known as a traumatic event.

Trauma refers to death or injury events or the possibility of death or serious injury. Trauma includes incidents of high intensity or a level of suffering that would not be able to cope with any human being. The term TRAUMA is generally reserved for:

Natural disasters: hurricanes, floods, volcanic events, fires, and all-natural catastrophes.

Man-made catastrophes like war or fight, prison or war camp experiences, physical assaults, sexual assaults, and other forms of victimization like robbery, mugging, invasion of your homeland involving a life threat or a limb.

Certain types of incidents that may be regarded as trauma could include a community and job tragedy, where a significant incident is involved, the death of a co-worker(s), chemical spills, or vehicular incidents involving vehicles, planes, train accidents or the death or attack of someone else.

Someone is in a traumatic event when they realize or suspect that someone around you could be killed or injured. Just like if you were mugged, for example, and they were telling you that if you did not do what they were saying, you have every reason to believe you are in danger. This incident can certainly be considered trauma. But if the mugger did not say a word, even made other facial expressions or gestures to hurt or assassinate you. You can also be traumatized for any reason you think you may be seriously injured or murdered during a robbery.

Just list the circumstances or experiences that can be called "traumatic," which cannot be described as trauma, which brings us to this question, "what are these circumstances and experiences together?" A traumatic event or circumstance that does not reflects your usual experience or perceptions about how the world works and how others treat each other.

Situation and situations can be upsetting because they contradict the perception of what is meant to be and why in the world. This can disrupt yourself and others ' sense. This can break the illusion that your world is secure and that you have control over your life. When trauma is taught by someone else, it may have an effect on your trust in others, making it very difficult to have relationships with other people and also affect your self-esteem and self-worth. In the days and weeks following the traumatic event, almost everyone will undergo special sequestration; the long-lasting and more destructive consequences will indicate that a diagnosable disorder may have evolved for psychological and emotional functioning.

Psychiatrists and psychologists have established two (2) types of traumatic stress

    Acute Stress Disorder
    A Post Traumatic Stress Disorder (PTSD)

Acute stress disorder is when symptoms progressed within four weeks of the traumatic event and did not last LONGER THAN FOUR (4) WEEKS.

Post-traumatic stress disorder (PTSD), which is frequently referred to as types made with almost the same symptoms, but the distinction between them is how long the traumatic event took place and the symptoms.

Post-traumatic stress disorder has symptoms formed in LONGER THAN FOUR (4) weeks following the traumatic event as the LONG AS SIX (6) months.

TRAUMA STRESSORS OF LIFE SKILLS

Healthcare professionals may be disconcerted when trauma survivors come after rehabilitation and find out about the symptoms recurring after reassessment.

Trauma is really a serious assault on the functioning of human life.

Which happens to a regular daily task such as paying the bills or resolving problems, so it all suddenly appears to be a gigantic feat?

Could the negative emotions or physical symptoms have been triggered a day or two before or after a vacation gathering, and the survivor remembers an unpretentious moment that surfaces?

Trauma refers to people who have experienced a distressing psychological and life-risk event. A person who has suffered an injury, wounds, sickness, physical, mental, emotional or sexual abuse or other crimes, an individual who is a veteran of war, a military officer or a displacement refugee who comes out of war or a violent country, a search-and-rescue worker may happen, a survivor of natural disasters, or a traumatic event bystander.

A survivor may rekindle moments of fear, shame, regret, anger, or life disillusionment.

A traumatic event may cause feelings that cause tiredness, low energy, crying, or lack of focus or impatience. Explosions of rage occur for no cause. The recollection of trauma is burning and hallucinations and it can be so intense that normal life is difficult to live.

It is known to a trauma survivor, assumption that healing has happened, and rehabilitation has ended with chaos in mind. Thoughts, emotions, and feelings are irritated. Symptoms return to cause distress without warning. It becomes overwhelming to be able to manage a basic home or work activities.

Be alert to know and understand destructive emotions that may occur following opposition are essential tools for life skills.

Self-consciousness and self-treatment are arsenals of trauma-episodic memory.

Life suddenly can crash because images, conversations, smells, or sounds begin to remind us of something that was now associated with a traumatic event at that time.

The risk of successful treatment improves if other disorders are correctly diagnosed and treated.

It is a continuous process that explains coping with traumatic stress. He states that if we know the consequences of trauma, we will help our loved ones more (to ourselves).

Life skills can allow people to draw on a wide array of problem-solving strategies to address their career, home, or social challenges. The degree to which a person with trauma incorporates life actions after trauma is a measure of success and requires great support.

During recovery from trauma, people learn during their healing to recognize feelings of denial, to be involved, to find support, to face the causes, and to ground after a flashback.

Trauma survivors must take time to treat the feelings of the experience and know how to find a time to be alone or find someone to share the experience with the family or friends. You need to realize that expressing your knowledge without judgment is welcomed.

The goal is to understand that trauma will occur at different times of the year.

The best approach to trauma by discovering a number of ways to normalize it, by not being depressed or fearful of symptoms and difficulties. (Unlike catastrophic thoughts like, "I am back to myself, it's happening again," and emphasizing coping strategies, such as being involved, loving, seeking social support).

Family members and friends care deeply but hold faiths that should heal rapidly. This can delay the recovery of a trauma survivor. Advocating "life is too short" and "stop focusing on the past–end it."

Healing takes time, and for everyone, it is special.

Family physicians believe that it is an essential part of a life's ability to understand and express feelings, deal with trauma-related frustration and safeguard thought processes so as not to weaken the capacity to cope on a daily basis.

Consciousness is important.

Emotional injuries take time to heal, or may never heal in certain cases.

Emotions from a traumatic event will take years, and it is a gross awakening when they do. A revelation explores the experience and the pain associated with it. What can happen is a reminder of more pain that adds to the initial trauma. Once this happens, the survivor needs recovery time to work through it and get ready to get better for it on the other end.

Trauma may cause ongoing self-esteem issues. This affects simple life skills management. Trauma is harder for some than others to heal. Many continue to inspire others to reach the dark stage of a journey that transforms their lives.

The effect of trauma on the whole person and the spectrum of psychological issues must be discussed. Restoration occurs when the person is ready to move past the pain.

Symptoms come back like a flashback in a movie trailer, in bits and pieces it can subside.

By being prepared to listen, we can help a loved one with post-traumatic stress. Choose a time when both of you are comfortable for debate.

It can take months, years, and decades during the recovery from trauma. PTSD never leaves for some.

Trauma affects the ability of a person to handle basic skills in life. This is generally necessary for understanding the world or having the resources to create a fulfilling life. Daily tasks, school or work, building relationships, or personal feelings of association or connection are clearly overwhelming.

The signs of trauma hinder the desire to live to the fullest.

Many treatments for PTSD are available to meet the survivor's unique needs.

Everyone is different so that a PTSD treatment can work for one person and can't work for another.

Life coaching is available to support listening-without fixing but helping to solve those strong feelings, including embarrassment, frustration, or guilt. A life coach can offer strategies to help plan beyond PTSD and work towards achieving life goals based on a new human working method.

A life skills approach to trauma involves finding a new balance of personal life. Bridging new wall of understanding and self-discovery during a trauma recovery means learning to live with a new skills management agenda. It is worth commitment to spend time learning what works best when recovering from the effects of trauma.

Abandonment is not a choice, but finding self-love and understanding, or having the required assistance, brings additional accomplishments to a survivor's particularly brave life, with the stresses of past trauma.

SURVIVING TRAUMA

What is trauma? Many of us are different, but the core feelings are the same. Fear, rage, retirement, frustration, intimidation are all emotional elements of the traumatic survivors. It can be a life-long process that requires all kinds of coping skills to deal successfully with it. I don't talk about physical trauma, I'm talking about psychological trauma, but one may lead to another.

Emotional trauma increased the feeling of shame many years ago. Families hid it and never spoke about it, fear that trauma would shed disgraceful light on the survivor. The syndrome of' we don't air our dirty laundry.' Blocking the incident was the only way to treat the accident, but it did not solve the problem, of course. It was encouraged to learn to remove or to disassociate from the recollection of the incident, but it only removed intense negative emotions and made the survivor live a wounded life. The myriad of emotions associated with overcoming trauma can never stop. And when these emotions are dismissed, they reappear in the form of self-destructive behavior.

This was particularly true of soldiers who experienced war horror. The circumstances leading to death and serious injury were so devastating that the mind could not comprehend the magnitude of the situation. Years after this incident, if not handled, reminder event caused them to live their trauma history over and over again and think it was occurring again. Their desire to never achieve peace became a clinical medical problem in the psychiatric community, and a new approach to therapy was discovered — post-traumatic stress disorder (PTSD).

We use our survival skills to deal with the trauma and ensure self-preservation (although it may not seem like we did at that time). It is the implications that generate serious difficulties in our thought and behavior. Repression, as I said, is typically the first condition. We use this as a defense mechanism, but this typically can not last forever. At a time when the individual cannot perform well in everyday life circumstances in society, the question must be dealt with carefully. Recurring nightmares, panic attacks, anxiety, addiction, and depression, combined with repression, can consume one's life. The decision to cope with the traumatic event is a significant achievement, and difficult research can only then begin. It is not an easily made decision. The victim learns that she really is a survivor, driven by a trained mental health professional. This change of perspective paves the way for the rest of the job. In a safe environment, it is important to address the specifics of trauma. A therapist can rate and recognize the amount of information revealed when the survivor is overwhelmed. In some cases, the balance is delicate, but the therapist will usually take advantage of the patient in the expectation that the whole incident can be handled in time.

I always prevent those sitting alone on a computer from reliving their trauma, since the exposure will devastate them, and there is no safety net to fall into. I understand the human need, but emotional well being must be taken into account. A therapist tells an anxious client that the pain does not exist. The incident has happened in the past, and the customer is not necessarily at risk. This is very valuable for the customer as they know that they talk of the past without the danger of repeating it. The aim of therapy is not to remove pain from the customer mind but rather to make memories easier to manage, to avoid them being depressed, or their quality of life is ruined. Discussing the event regularly helps to reduce the emotional power, the customer feels traumatized at first. Speaking to other people who have had trauma and sharing their emotions can be very helpful in support groups and reassure the person that they are not alone. When the trauma no longer affects the survivor's life, they are free to appreciate the good aspects of their lives. We all want to have the best life, and learning to handle past traumatic events can save our lives.

Note that during this cycle, you are kind to yourself. You didn't ask. We are all fragile human beings, feeling alone sometimes is our history, so it takes to love and patience. There is nobody who wants to live in terror. We want to live in sunlight and recover our lives and connections. It is never necessary that traumatic events of the past should dominate our lives indefinitely. We learn to be the leader in the aftermath of our crisis. We can live with the knowledge that our trauma is behind us and that we can have the kind of life we want. Everything is possible.

CHAPTER TWO

THE AFTERSHOCKS OF TRAUMA

If trauma could be equated to the earthquake, it has many effects, most of which have an effect on a person during the remainder of his or her life and can be called his or her aftermath.

1. Trauma is an automatic reaction to a protection or survival threat. It's a mark on the brain that contributes to its reactivation by its intrinsic neuroplasticity or its capacity to reconnect its millions of neurons.

The amygdala, two almond-shaped nuclei in the limbic system at the end of the hippocampus serves as the brain's "smoke detector", which constantly monitors the imminent danger, though that hazard is just about an approximation to a decades ago counter-survival or threatening event. It gets information and processes it much quicker than the upper neocortex section, and when it sees even a hint of what has already been shown to be harmful, it activates its combat-flight-freeze mechanisms, which generate high levels of stress hormones that allow the central nervous system to respond and prepare people to act appropriately to improve their survival. The threat can be real or perceived, current, or literally released from the past. Primed and pumped, they are fitted with a high oxygen supply, and increased heart rate, and increased blood pressure to combat or avoid the threat.

Although traditional memories can be broken, the traumas and their physiological effects are retriggered, and preserved as frozen, fragmented bits, not cohesive connections telling a particular story. This trigger will reach the proportions of the hairpin.

A person can move physically and intellectually, but he will remain emotionally attached to it unless his trauma is resolved and integrated. It creates a duality between present and past as if he had to put one foot at a time.

Trauma contributes to a transition. It removes the driver from his seat and makes him a passenger, harnesses the extraordinary power to direct his life and destroy it, and brings into the present the deteriorating effects that have accrued in the past.

In The Body Keeps the Score: Brain, mind, and body in the cure of trauma, "nothing could make sense for people living a trauma, they are caught in a death or a life situation, blind rage, or paralyzing fear." The brain reacts exactly as it did during the initial event and deludes the person into thinking that there is trauma at that very moment and that there was a passage of time between the first events. "The brain and mind are continually anxious, as though they were in imminent danger.

Most parts of the world continue to be seen and perceived by trauma through frequent retriggering, which can lead to almost constant mental, physical, emotional, and physiological feelings. This results, of course, in the utter distortion of the truth of a human.

Immersed in the past, the mind is trying to defend itself from the current approaches.

Traumas do not look like tales with beginnings, intermediates, and ends. Alternatively, they give only in the form of hallucinations, fragmented images, sides, fragments, body sensations, delusions, and bursts of disconnected panic and terror non-interpretable indications of their origin.

"Dissociation is the source of trauma" (ibid, p. 66). "The traumatic experience is separated and scattered in order for feelings, sounds, images, perceptions, and physical sensations associated with (it) to exist by themselves. The sensory memory fragments enter the present where they are resurrected literally. Until the trauma is overcome, it is the stress hormones the body hides to defend itself, and the protection begins to circulate. In an effort to escape the pain, which he may not actually recognize, and the emotional storm inside him, he can use any method to decrease it, whether it be the actual fleeing acts he determines or sweating it up with alcohol and drugs.

One of the confusion of trauma is that an original experience leads to the failure to record the time of the event; thus, when it is later reactivated, the person cannot put it in chronological, differentiated perspectives by realizing that, "This happened to me when I was five.

The more traumas the individual is caused, the more he becomes trapped in his past and the less alive and absorbed in his present. Without intervention, therapy, or participation in a 12-step program, it becomes a snowball gathering. In reality, the more power it exercises and the more its constant grasp on the past retains. They capture and overload the individual when he loses his own life, firstly when he witnessed his original life-threatening incident and secondly when he experiences the flood of stress hormones and volatile emotions.

This describes one of the behavioral characteristics of an adult baby. This shows that a child is a reactor rather than an actor as he suddenly startles and stirs as his responses crisscross the span of time between the age of his initial and current trauma. It also takes a large part of his life because he does all he can to prevent the unbearable sensations he is exposed to, to stop that which triggers him, including taking full isolation.

A person gets hit in battle or flight mode basically as though a button on a machine was depressed but cannot disengage.

But traumatic experiences leave traces with dark secrets unnoticeably passed down over generations.' "We track our minds and bodies, our capacity to rejoice and affection, and even to our genetics and immune systems." It's likely never again that an individual will be the same unless they're tackled and solved.

2. Trauma Aftershocks: While traumas tend to disappear after the danger has been over, they are not relegated to the' missing and forgotten' file despite what the individual may believe. Nevertheless, as a cauldron dropped into a pool, trauma triggers the effect of fighting, assault, and violence on those who are exposed. It is not only all-encompassing and oppressive but also deletes a person with present power and makes him as powerless as he used to be when the original incident occurred.

Traumas lie dormant, but not disabled in self-system, there are like an emotional bomb waiting to explode for the right person or relationship to activate, they are triggered and they will be aimed at the person or whatever has acted as the trigger, and for a moment the wound has a voice, maybe not the right voice, but the only voice in which it knows how.

Immediately and unpretentiously exposed to a dangerous occurrence or person, actual or perceived, causing intense anxiety, horror, and helplessness, unable to defend or protect themselves, hallucinations, nightmares, and intense and distracting emotions. Although he was able to survive his initial trauma decades earlier, he never recovered from it entirely, as the memories are repeated endlessly in his reorganized nervous system.

The more it is triggered, the more it becomes automatic until the person is trapped and mired in the brain replay. While its neocortex or emotional portion constantly reacts and causes havoc, it does not notify a logical pre-frontal cortex portion of what danger it is or may actually be because, in the main, it suspends its rationality and overtakes it. It essentially commands that person, "Do what I want and do not think about it!" Freud regarded the unrelenting reconstruction of trauma survivors as "compulsions to repeat." Although the PTSD symbols are equal to the activation of a powerful shell to make a burning building, its water continues to spread after the fire was extinguished, and cannot be stopped until the building itself drowns out. What begins as help ends as harm, and if an individual does not harm or kill the original threat, his unchecked brain, albeit at night, will.

The only remaining link between the original and reactivated trauma are physiological stimuli, the strength or repetitive reactivation of which has already occurred.

an alienation from others and the environment. Always thinking that he is looking beyond, he is isolated from others, despite what might be near physical closeness, due to his lack of belief and repressed fears, this consist of the bottled damage he was suffering from, but could not recover, and the likelihood of drug toxins transmitted to him that are still circulating through his blood without his knowledge.

"They are the deadwood of repressed unconsciousness, unresolved rage, desperation and desire," "When an unconscious person is called to contain all this in unrecognized silence, there is little breathing space for lightness and serenity, which belongs to the higher consciousness. When parents grew up under the same dysfunctional, violent, abusive, and intoxicated circumstances, they produced for their children, and they may only have been present physically. Prisoners may leave their children to understand why, but still very lost, to their own addictions and unexplained upbringings.

False and ineffective, they struggled to foster the growth of their children, enabling them to mimic or tap into outlets without adequate parental models.

Self-Image is generated by focusing on a person's parents, resulting in their beliefs, perceptions, emotions, and thoughts being internalized. For starters, if a father says, "My son is nothing worthless," he will believe it. The older, more mature adult knows certainly better, "explains him. The abuse of any of his emotional, mental, physical, and sexual aspects leads to a loss of innocence for the child and fails to produce the requisite confidence that could allow him to navigate the world as a grown-up person eventually. Their problem is also compounded by their assumption that only one person or solution can fix it, leading it to fail inevitably. Yet they can't look without filling up the inside. Their wounds warrant healing, internal rehabilitation, and eventual return to wholeness, not an external source of the future. For example, the buying of a new car often creates transient emotional increases or enthusiasm about the object, but it soon wears off and causes it to collapse into its lower state, as though it folds into itself. Trauma survivors are prone to reactivation. To describe or grasp his psychologically unpredictable and debilitating reactions, he becomes a bystander, often incapable of reaching the middle of them. Like a tenth-power exponential equation, his traumas repetitively accumulate more energy and cause the person to fall into his past fast sand unless the person's roots have been found and removed by desensitization or Higher Power dissolution.

Failure to do so will cause the person to work against detrimental defenses that do not necessarily exist at this time and re-generate the same disruption in the attachment bond that took place during the initial threat. He will only repel them instead of attracting and communicating with others.

Those that grew up with guilt, malpractice, and violence, subconsciously, find others to be "figures of authority," or those who are now the representatives of the father, who immediately rekindle his unresolved past, causing him to panic, fade and revert to childhood impotence as he redefines and uses the tactics he takes to protect himself.

A father whose traumas are unresolved is guided by his infant; pressuring him to do something, whilst the child himself, unable to understand or defend or to prevent violence, only believes that his lack of ability to provide service and lack of ability to love are the justified culprits of harmful behavior. It will most likely reinforce the chain by establishing another link in the generational relation before he takes corrective action as an adult.

He had no alternative. He had no choice.

For many children, it is easier to dislike themselves rather than threaten their relationship with their parents by expressed frustration or fleeing, Thus, abused children are likely to grow up thinking they are inherently unlovable, only in this way will their young minds understand why they have been treated so badly. Dictated his' childhood program,' which taught subtly him to not trust during episodes of not predictable deception and any number and combination of forms of abuse, he was unable to lay the foundations that others seemed to have easily achieved. He had no choice but to put his defensive radar very high.

It could eventually relegate him to the abuser's or authority figure of the equation in a moment of particularly high fear, causing him to accuse the individual with whom it interacts with the overwhelming guilt, rage, criticism, and blame.

This projection of pain, another after-shake trauma, emanates from wounds too deep or coarse to accepted, thereby shifting the burden to another human. In essence, his trauma is a break with truth, trust, faith, hope, and positive expectations of the self.

Unless it is cured, the interpretation created by children will always be associated with adulthood, and its logic, reasoning, and maturity can not necessarily sever or oppose it.

If, for example, he has concluded that his abuse has arisen from a deserved punishment even when he is an adult, he will continue to feel that his abuse is inferior and still worthy of such treatment because of his faulty, inadequate composition.

As his defenses have been developed to protect him from danger and encourage some degree of peace, he disconnects from his true feelings, another aftershock trauma.

Carried into adulthood, when they are just unquestioned parts of him, his defenses are integral to his personality and manifest as the subconsciously employed survival characteristics of adults created by his brain, which was forced to restructure itself to survive and cope in a volatile, unstable home environment.

The adult syndrome itself is one of the main trauma aftershocks. The person entering life in such a weakened state is an incompletely developing, maturity-arrested child, and often is reduced to early life reactions and defenses.

Another aftershock is the failure to feel or even imagine safe and meaningful intimacy. Since trauma itself is an abrupt disconnection from another and reality, the pure thinking, although mostly in a subconscious state, reactivates its elements, causes the individual to reject them, shuts them down emotionally, or braves him uncomfortably. But he does not understand why he cannot completely relax and interact with another person on a soul-to-soul level.

A half of him desires it while another half is scared and refuses it. In the latter case, it is nothing more than a trauma that reverts profoundly into the mind of the person. It warns with an emotional attitude: "You know what happened to you for the first time in direct, inextricable contact with your abuser!"

Traumas are constantly reappearing. Since they have their own strength, they are not ignored or reburied, and they always come up with ways of expressing themselves, such as dreams or reenactments. These reactions can occur within, cause extreme, and ultimately physiologically endangering manifestations of health, or without, animated, abuser-emulating behavior.

It is impossible to underestimate the depth of repressed, untreated trauma reaching the cellular level, which enables them to elicit painful, physical sensations. Abusive adolescence leads to adult relationships, "turning to mines that cause bursts of emotion." Adult stress is a catalyst for replays of childhood as if the individual has returned to his or her early life.

The person, once again threatened, may immediately replay his childhood defenses to "overcome" the perceived threat.

The failure to mourn casualties sufficiently is another big aftershock. Because he may have been forced to isolate unpleasant or intolerable thoughts and feelings into a part of the brain outside his consciousness, he cannot process them entirely, mentally, contributing to his unfinished sorrow.

Another aftershock is the compulsion of repetition. Beyond an individual's consciousness, his brain repeats experiences and episodes so that he can finally understand, overcome, and assess what he was unable to do during the first traumatic events he was subjected to.

Child abuse is, to some extent, the product of the brain trying to end what has been done to another human.

Nevertheless, trauma is more than just recorded incidents and emotional sparks and attempts to survive his lifetimes threatened times. Whatever is experienced in children becomes a cell-printed script, allowing a person to search for another significant circumstance or event which, despite the fact that it might be dysfunctional or abusive, closely approximates the plot with which he is most familiar. This phenomenon, along with the need to finish what the brain has endured, allows an intoxicated individual who is treated as an adult to be drawn by a behavior pattern, allowing him to "make it right this time" or correct in the partner what he feels he or she was called for, but he or she has not been called upon to do with his or her dysfunctional parent. But it didn't work then, and it won't work now.

The wound aftershock can be known as the tendency for treatment. Reload or attempt to relieve emotional pain, and a person may boost it by projecting it onto others and then providing care and support as an outward effort to mitigate one's own wounds.

Whereas a person may desperately need meaningful relationships and privacy, his cross-border and accepted childhood has deprived him of any sense of self-sufficiency and identity, yet another trauma. Healthy relationships are based on co-states, where both members visit. If the upbringing of an individual does not model this phenomenon, he will only conceptualize intimacy as a merger, capture, loss of his own identity, and codependency unconsciously. The safeguards shield him from what he thinks will be inextricable and smooth intertwined.

Certain post-shock symptoms include anxiety, neurosis, codependence, and addictions. Trauma survivors perform regular behavior, such as eating and functioning, in an odd and unnatural fashion so that they show their true self and establish a temporary state of calm. But both are transient and self-perpetuating, which leads to acts that can damage the individual, as happens with over dosage of drugs or alcohol. Unlike band-aids, they will hide the wound temporarily, but they do nothing to repair it.

While victims of abuse may be motivated and driven to see issues addressed by mental health professionals, they can only end up relying on something that the individual once considered his or her remedies. As the tip of the iceberg, they just sought to numb and avoided what they were driven by.

Unfelt feelings that are simply held back until they are addressed do not decline over time.

Another important trauma aftershock is a loss of confidence in the person, as one of the manifestations of trauma is the inability to control or even to predict his reactivating times.

He can only be physically present, emotionally numb and isolated and separated by a strong, impenetrable wall, placing one foot ahead of the other, but seldom experience a real part of life.

Detached to a certain degree from the present, it replays the traumas of its history but overlaps them with current conditions and the present and often misinterprets them and repels them with defenses of security.

"It is vital difficult for traumatized people to discover if they really are safe and if they are in danger will activate their defenses," says Van der Kolk (Op Cit., p. 85).

His inner world can be messy emotionally. If a person is in survival mode, even as an adult, they will most likely feel continually drained and tired and subjected to a dangerous physiological and emotional reaction. Self-care and dietary needs can become compromises because they can sometimes ignore them.

The brain trauma response mechanism may have worked to increase a person's chances of survival during the first incident but works against him, particularly for wrong reasons, when he becomes tangled with the inner turmoil.

An individual can be so inextricably bound to the fears of retriggered trauma that he becomes the living example of "this is only thing that we had to fear is fear itself." While the threatened and scared seek others for connective help, comfort, and protection, those who have been abused mistrust them to provide such restorative connections and these "other" can be an inevitable and confounding source of their trauma triggers.

Confidence in parents or primary caregivers is only shown that people will most probably follow suit later in life because of chronic treachery, negligence, abandonment, or violence and the lack of regularity in which a child has been able to meet its needs.

"Children with abuse and neglect stories know that their fear, begging and crying don't register with their caretakers," Nothing they can do or say helps or attracts attention and help. They have the condition that they give up when they face challenges in their later life. "Fearing further retaliation and punishment, the victims of abuse remain silent and private and never discuss their worries and concerns with others and encourage their anger to smolder, which, in adulthood, can lead to an infinite numbers of physical, emotional and psychological disorders."They have no alternative but to organize themselves to live within the communities they have. We have no other authority to turn and help, unlike adults. Their parents are the authorities. "Chronic exposure to the trauma, as happens in the abused home environment of children, sparks continuous retriggers which are closing the gap between them until calmer and safer times are no longer reachable. Later in life, those who remind them of themselves become the figure of authority that retriggers them. Fear of losing control; always alert to risk and rejection; self-loathing, flashbacks; fog which prevents you from remaining at work and engaging in... The fear of losing control always; as reactivated emotions become emotionally and psychologically overwhelming, these stimuli can function as dual-direction polarities. Like a person jumping over the fence, he can either re-success them and fall backward, or use them to recognize their source, address them, desensitize, understand, solve their problems.

CODEPENDENCY AND TRAUMA

You will make important steps to resolve codependency through the development of new behaviors, skills, and actions. However, deeper recovery can involve trauma, usually, that started in infancy. Trauma can be social, physical, or environmental, from fire to emotional neglect. Childhood experiences have had a greater impact on you than now because you had no adult coping skills. Codependents often suffer more traumas due to relationships with others who are abandoned, abusive, addicted, or mentally ill as a result of their growth in a dysfunctional family environment.

Childhood Trauma can be traumatic if accidental, fragile, and genuine cannot be safe. It is emotionally harmful if you were dismissed, shamed, or disciplined for sharing your thoughts or feelings or because you were young, deficient, or required. Many people are neglected, discarded emotionally, or physically, and believe that they can not trust or trust anyone. You hide your real child, and you play the role of an adult before you are ready. Divorce, disease, or death of a parent or sibling, depending on how parents treated it, can also be traumatic. Events are dangerous when they are chronic or extreme in such a way that the limited ability of a child to deal with what is happening overwhelms.

The wounds are how you had these encounters. Some of them all grow up, but the marks remain and compensate for relationships and life issues. Deeper healing means that these wounds must be opened again, cleaned, and the treatment of compassion added.

Trauma symptoms are subjective and vary from person to person. That child in a family responds to the same experience and trauma differently. Symptoms may come and go and may not appear until years after the incident.

You do not need to experience all of the following symptoms from trauma:

> Over-react to stimuli that are reminder of trauma avoid thinking, remembering or talking about causes for trauma
> Stop things you once had
> Feeling hopeless about the future
> Experience memory deficits or unable to recall parts of trauma
> Have difficulty concentrating
> Have problems

Diagnosis calls for a variety of signs that last for at least 30 days and can begin long after a triggering event. The main signs include intrusion thoughts in dreams, bursts of waking, and repeated negative thinking. Prevent trauma triggers like sleep ignoring or avoiding emotions or ignorance Hyper arousal placing the nervous system alert, causing irritability, exhaustion, and difficulty relaxing and sleeping. A person often has many traumas, leading to more serious symptoms, including mood swings, depression, high blood pressure, and chronic pain.

The ACE (Adverse Children's Experience) study found a direct connection between adult and childhood trauma symptoms. ACE cases assessed were:

Mother Treaties
Family Mental Illness
Parental Separation or Divorce
Member of a prisoner's family
Emotional Neglect

Some forms of traumatic events include:

Betrayal
Training or living with an alcoholic (normally involving emotional abuse)
Death and alcohol abuse
Chronic obstructive pulmonary disease
Depression
Fetal mortality
Health-related quality of life
Drug use
Chemical heart disease
Liver disease
Poor work results
Financial burden
Health-related intimate partner violence

The risk of spouse and partner violence is higher than in the participant's susceptibility to following conditions: Curative trauma is like going back in time and remembering something which has not been conveyed, reviewing dysfunctional values and actions again, and familiarizing you with the missing parts. The first step in recovery is to face what has happened. Some people deny their trauma in childhood, particularly when they are growing up in a stable setting. If your parents weren't violent, just unresponsive, you'd still experience depression, denial, and guilt about yourself and your emotions that you might have rejected or ignored fully. The new experience, feeling, and talking about what happened are important elements of the healing process. This is "emotional abandonment." Another step in healing is to lament about what you lost. Stages of grief include frustration, sadness, negotiation, often remorse, and acceptance. Acceptance does not mean you agree with what happened, but without anger or intense feelings, you are more rational about it. When you expel your past feeling, you have more energy and motivation to invest in your future.

During the process and it is too often omitted and it is essential that you discern false convictions, as a result of trauma, and replace healthier ones. These are typically shameful attitudes resulting from childhood shameful messages and experiences. Recovery also involves understanding and improving the relationship and talking to yourself, leading to undesirable results and behavior.

TRAUMA IS TRANSFORMED

You die when you read it. You die. You're always giving birth to something when you complete it. The human body has about 75 trillion cells. Every cell has a particular task and life span. Until "us," they die and are replaced by new cells. We survive us, too, when a person dies, their cells take another day before they are all dead. We are actually in the state of an ongoing resurrection where parts of us die are replaced by parts of us who are born. Not surprisingly, I'm not the same guy that I was last year.

The skin is your soul's tattoo. That's what we cover, ink, pinch, poke and caress, but what you felt about three weeks ago is different than what you are currently feeling. Your baby may feel good a month ago, but if it's picked up from the ward or hurried, it's a bit annoying. The skin has improved, but the brain is mature, obstinate, and reptile because it likes horde memories. The skin is shed, and the brain is retained. Surely both are necessary, but they work against each other. If they worked in tangent, the skin's durability would teach the brain to let go after it has absorbed the same terms a million times. In return, the brain would remind the skin to stay a little longer, before it is released, to read what is written on its old skin.

I also help patients by first stimulating their senses so that the influence of abuse claims has vanished. Often I continue with the body's largest organ, the blood and the skin. Touch, read it, and remember, there's something you can know about trauma and resilience. When a person thinks of trauma, they remember the dignified feeling of stupor that fills their skin with disgust. Many victims of sexual abuse say they feel filthy, offensive, and disgusting. It is not the same skin that the offender touched a year ago and that they cannot touch their skin. At the psychic level, your skin you're touching now isn't the same skin that the abuser is touching. It was removed and replaced by a new jacket. This is good news for all, from addiction to old feelings. It's a clever organ that wipes away other fingerprints. Yet the skin does not like snakes that are smarter than its coiled brain. The memory of this laceration is rooted in the mind when aggression lacerates the skin. The brain's regeneration is much slower. Many people say that it does not regenerate its cells; others say yes, but slower than anywhere else in the body. Only know that while they work it out, it isn't exactly the most appropriate for shedding. After all, it's the library. It's best to arrange or shake the pages.

Although you must master the spirited mind if you want to master your soul, the chambers enjoy playing skin games. The catch-22 evokes the worst images and returns to your new skin. It is not your abuser; therefore, who touches you now; it is your messy memories that torture your skin. You are tormenting.

Worse still, memory can become so suffocating that you suffer from amnesia and don't remember anything. When you know that the causes are those which are embedded in the fallen skin, a portion of the "letting go" will occur, yet simply "letting go" always calls for memories, or you will become the root of your suffering and never turn torment into art.

The skin has to throw away; the mind has to order itself. PTSD-related anxiety that is too common for victims of abuse occurs as thoughts clash in each other to make themselves heard in the crowded room of your chambers. The memories merge, and the trauma takes place before you know it and turns it all into a catalyst, including good memories. The flashback comes in, and even the scent of your favorite fragrance is soaked in the feces of the beast that overtakes your thoughts. A trauma tyrant overthrows your entire mind, restricting all movement until your skin is dead.

Okay, this crazy dance isn't pointless. What you've just done is carry the brain to the skin. They need each other, but they act like strangers in their own divorced body. You've got to link them. How? How? Now the spirit approaches who is wiser than both, and instructs you not to let go of the trauma. It only changes you. The brain doesn't change, but the way it says memory changes. Like oil, it just changed shape and went somewhere else. This critical device, which is called active detachment, is the strongest reasoning and emotion to function in.

Take care because avoidance is not an active detachment, but can make you feel like it is because it gives a false sense of strength to the ego.

The narration, as well as the visual arts technique, is often used by me to allow the victim to re-tell her story as many times as she wants, thereby manipulating the pen by withdrawing it from the hands of the uninvited colonist. Add to it the realm of dreams and the imagination of an existentialist, and you have an initial idea. Viktor Frankl was saved from the insanity of concentration camps by imagination, so he learns this type of computed imagination. He was rooted in ovens, but he was active in Zen, which enabled him to see reality without fear. His imagination could have thrown him into the inferno of disassociation and delusion, without this brilliant calculation. Rather, he refined it to build and construct whole schools of thought like most masters. He remembered every aspect of the camp and still managed to rise above it by his inner ensemble with the most impressive chamber music that we hear about his years after his death.

He understood that memory is split into two places: the actual and the illusion. For instance, violence is real; but the strength of soul attackers is not real. A soul is better because it is not targeted. It is the breath of God that you hold. See: Breath is the ancient Hebrew word Ruach-the spirit of God. If this soul finds expression in every human being's body, it is funneled into every individual. What fills us is called Nafesh; the spirit of God embodied in form as breath. You see, no human being can carefully manage a breath of divinity; therefore, wisdom demands that life forms be freely given to pursuing the dream of the eternal soul. Without the connection of everything, we are unformed and cannot be a whole being, but a part or breath. Each of us has a part of that soul within us. The soul does not split because it is not ours, but all of us. Like Sisyphus, we try to chain death and lock our soul in our cages, but it escapes.

It's not yours alone when it's gone. This emerges from the heavens and returns to the stars. When an old star dies, it pours its light and pours its death ashes into a new star's formation. Dust to dust might very well mean "stardust to stardust." Therefore, trauma doesn't seem so daunting when we see something that we don't know, but that which we don't know.

Maybe the explosion you hear on this planet can sound like a soul breaking, but not. It's the lie that you hear. The lie that the brain says knows who we are and tricks us into using it to lure us with a lot of information. The lie is the over-touched skin that lets us rejuvenate with a new skin, but forgets (thanks to the forgetful mind and hastily old skin) to give us the code to do so.

The split that we hear is not the spirit, but the illusion that suggests that we are the tomb of the sins of others: silence before or injustice after the crime scene. The cry between you is the gavel of your character and the rise of your answer. The traumatized could and should be the teller of the truth. When the illusion of innocence is shattered, the trauma is transformed. Everyone is a thief, and the victim is only she or he who screams in utter terror, only at that moment. To live there, we must scream forever through stitched mouths. We didn't rescue us at that time, and so now they have to save their dignity. Not just for them, but for us all.

So you see, trauma long ceased to be a burden I wear alone. I am generous and will make sure I never enter the house without a gift selectively deaf, stupid, and blind. Trauma breaks mind and body and not the soul, who can remember light-years of information and be sufficiently agile to release illusions from it.

The irony is that our traumas are actual, but not ours. Let them go means let them go so that you are not the cryptographer of all our trespasses, trapped within the small body that once held secret vaults. Let it go. Let it go. It's a crime against HUMANITY and not a crime. You now understand why voicing your anguish is important? You, my darling, or I'm a tomb. Even the children who died in the name of the sins of your father are not buried. They're here. They're here. We're here. We're here. Make sure that your trauma invites everyone to the divine tribunal. Even death; the elderly teacher of trauma is present. Trauma is a small death, a little death.

Evocate creativity, reflected in your art, work, and life, so that the perpetrator is called out quietly and clearly. When you wait for a dysfunctional human court to determine what is fair, you won't die. You will become a dream that will never leave its body and have the same recurring nightmares. Raise your standards until they are below you. There are many other ways of claiming that you don't rely on old institutions. Try and if they don't work, remember what knowledge has deepened, and worked and shed the rest with ignorance, the skin of the liquid oceans and pearled coils of wisdom needs more time to expand. This is a transformed trauma. Just forget nothing and shed it all.

COULD CHILD TRAUMA BEGIN BEFORE CONCEPTION?

This problem is much more complex than you could imagine. One of the complicating factors of the problem is that there is no description of what is traumatic, simple, and clearly defined. It is extremely late in what can be traumatic based on individual endurance and mental structures, but it doesn't mean it's naive and impossible to say with any certainty that this or that WILL contribute to trauma when you work with kids or families. Another complicating factor has become even more complex recently. In the field of biology, the epigenetic influences that can lead to changes within people are becoming more conscious. Epigenetic alteration is caused by environmental changes rather than by the transfer in DNA content in the genes. Such developments seem permanent and legacy for at least many generations.

Infinite and, in many respects, incalculable in nature are the variety and possibilities of environmental experiences. In this book, we discuss how anything that disrupts or interferes with a person's normal psychological, social, or emotional growth will lead to epigenetic changes through their descendants.

In order to deal with "when can trauma start" in this essay, the focus is on developing trauma? The trauma encountered by a mother before pregnancy will increase the probability of epigenetic effects on the behavior with her children. These results together indicate that trauma might occur and start for a child before it is born, based on the mother's life experience and stress levels. This is an important point to understand: That the mother's trauma or stress will build an epigenetic, environmental press or an atmosphere that has a negative impact on an disbelieve infant.

Trauma, injuries, inadequate neonatal care, or maternal medications can have severe effects on fetal development and generate novel brain patterns and sensitivities, which can later be reflected in uncommon or dysfunctional behaviors in children. Trauma may begin with the development of stressors that are significant in the lives of future mothers or with the functioning of the family and the ability of future mothers to cope with stressors.

Another complicating factor is the internal strength and adaptability of the mother when trauma starts. Not all experiences are equal; different people experience the same situations in an idiosyncratic or unique way, which challenges their ability to be definitive or absolute in determining where trauma was started. While the particular time may not be identifiable, there are factors that can intensify the trauma's effect on the mother and make trauma more likely. These are often known as the major acuity variables. INTENSITY, length, and frequency are these acuity variables. For the mother, these causes were the same as for the fetus or newborn child.

In an attempt to understand the start of trauma, one would like to understand how the mother perceives the intensity of the stressors. Most researchers refuse to use such a subjective variable because it is a challenge to create a good statistical analysis if everyone has a very individual and unique view of the strength of their work. It is a little easier to grasp and calculate the duration of time between the beginning and the end of an event, but even that is somewhat influenced by the expectations of the individual encounters stressors. The ultimate factor is how often something occurs that is stressful or distressing to the person who experiences it.

The interaction between FREQUENCY, INTENSITY, and DURATION becomes vitally important. You may have a low level of intensity, but if it lasts for long periods or happens quite often, it can start to produce tension that can theoretically overpower the capacity of your future mom to adapt or cope. If you had high intensity, long duration, and common events, the emotional, psychological, and, some extent, the physical resources of your future mother would be easily significantly devastated.

So when does trauma start? It can begin to manifest in the mother's life sometime before conception. This indicates that developing stable environments within a tolerable range of stresses before conception may well be a major factor in promoting healthy emotional and psychological growth among children significantly before conception. It is also possible that teenage mothers are at a higher risk of epigenetic disturbance in their offspring due to natural adolescence dysfunction.

A cautionary note should also be sounded; some readers might misunderstand the thrust of the author's thinking process. It must be stated clearly that the writer does not blame the mother for children problems, and that a future mother who is highly stressed, and who is exposed to an environment which overwhelms the ability of her to adapt, may lead to the epigenetic activation of infant trauma.

In short, a potential answer to the question of when trauma will start can be addressed in a postnatal manner by the mother's life and environment before she becomes pregnant by the stress level during pregnancy and by environmental problems. This should create a thinking process about how a healthy and inclusive community can be developed and sustained to enable unborn children to flourish and prosper.

CHAPTER THREE

THE METHOD OF PARENTING THE TRAUMATIZED CHILD

There are, sadly, many types of trauma experiences for children. The Trauma Education Resource for Children describes 14 forms of trauma, five of which are described here. The following seven clues take into account the five most common types of childhood trauma:

> Physical abuse, which occurs when a child is injured as a result of being struck, bruised, kicked, or shaken;
> Neglect, which occurs when the essential need of a child for food, clothes, shelter, medical attention, and education-is not met;
> Sexual assault occurs when a young child is involved in a sexual act by an adult or older child including exposure to pornography, groping, sexual intercourse and rape;
> Emotional abuse, including verbal abuse; and
> "Trauma caused by the program" as a result of a child being taken from home for foster care. It is important to be aware that it is only painful to have a child taken from home, placed in foster care, and separated from parents, siblings, and friends.

It is also important to know that as a caregiver, you are vital to the recovery of your child. You, as a parent or caregiver, are the support your child needs. If you are a parent of a traumatized infant, here are seven tips to help you understand the child. If the needs of your child are greater than you can manage, seek assistance from a mental health professional.

Tip #1: Know trauma symptoms and be watchful. Kids who have suffered abuse often have unexpected and drastic behavioral changes. You may not know how or if the behavior of your child has changed if you are a foster or adoptive parent or if the behavior you see is common for a child at their age. It is, therefore, important to listen when your child talks and watch its actions when it appears that he or she acts. Take note of prior, during, and after negative behaviors to determine the cause. If the negative behavior is excessive compared to the cause or if there seems to be no obvious reason, then the behavior could be traumatic. Some of the behavioral symptoms of trauma include irrational rage (picking, throwing, scratching, fighting), self-injury, unexplained anxiety, weeping without apparent reason, becoming overly anxious, easily depressed, or easily dismayed. Traumatized children are unable to react properly to normal, everyday circumstances. You must be trained. Kids are better taught by shaping the right way to do things.

Tips #2: Training pause. Regulations and consequences for breaking the rules will apply to every child. Because however, traumatized children are not sure of the right way, the best way to help them is to postpone discipline. Children of abuse may be physically and socially considerably younger than their biological age. These children may lack the social skills of another child of their age. Social skills are important to the healing process. Take the time to understand why your child acts like him or her and where the actions come from before determining how to discipline.

It may be effective in many cases to influence the action that your child wants to learn (Perry, 2001). You should speak to him or her by telling the child what you want him or her to do, instead of being punished. For example, if your child wants to play alone, it may need to be taught to share, or the child may take what he or she wants without requesting permission. A child who doesn't follow instructions doesn't necessarily have defiance but can demonstrate that the child is easily confused and unable to understand what he or she is asked about. When the child starts to learn these skills, the rules and consequences can be applied as problems arise.

Tip #3: Give your kids the options and let them decide. There is a sense of helplessness when children are abused or ignored. We soon learn that in these abusive situations, we have no influence and can be extremely anxious. In their lives, children need to have a sense of control. This helps to regain a child's sense of control, which helps to reinvigorate their mental and emotional growth. Your child is content because he or she has power by choosing what he or she wants.

Tip #4: Furnish structure. Trauma children often have an attachment problem. Change is difficult for children with attachment problems (Perry, 2001). This fact is critical for structure and routine. It is crucial for these children to have a set time for waking up in the morning, going to bed at night, and everything between them. It is also necessary to let them know if this plan is about to change in advance.

Tip #5: Create a cure climate. Children of abuse and neglect must feel safe, comfortable, and cared for. It is important to have a sense of being safe. Kids who lack support after a traumatic event struggle more than those who seek support from family or friends. If you are separated from your house, the protection is lost to make you feel helpless and alone. Such kids must know that someone cares what happens to them. It is therefore, important to help your child feel safe as a caregiver. The development of a safety plan is one way to help children who are sexually abused feel safe and secure. While this child may be an intruder at home, it is necessary to nurture, comfort, and love this child appropriately. These children must be loved unconditionally, as all children do.

Tip #6: Be a good audience. Don't push it if your child doesn't want to think about what it was like. Let the child lifts the matter on his own. Nonetheless, children often have to say and just be heard. Depending on the child's age, he or she may not even have to respond. However, be prepared to listen if your child wants to speak. The kid who talks of trauma is part of the process of healing. Allow children to express their feelings on their terms and in their own way. But don't judge, listen. Listen. It's important to believe your story. For situations where you are a foster parent or an adoptive parent, it is best not to ask questions since an investigation can be ongoing. Just listen. Just listen. You can nevertheless tell them that they were not responsible for what happened and that you were there to help them.

Tip #7: Seek therapeutic treatment. Children may not immediately show signs of trauma, but signs may occur sometime later. When distressed children remain untreated, their traumatized condition may interfere with their long-term growth. Traumatic children can be regressive, such as bedwetting when they have already been taught potty/toilet; or an older child behaving or talking like a kid who has just learned to speak. It is necessary to intervene early. Seek help from a professionally caring not only for your child but also for you so that you can properly adapt to the special needs of your child and avoid being frustrated.

Self-doubting would mean paralysis. It immobilizes and disables the patient, preventing him from taking steps in life. Think back to a time when you were optimistic about a goal, and the excitement began to slow down as the time came for the first move. That little voice inside your head began to say: Are you confident that you can?

What if you mess up? What happens?

Perhaps you must wait, perhaps you are not ready. As the days passed, you began to doubt the ability to accomplish the mission, and before long, things moved slowly. You feel stumped, stressed, like everybody's eye. Then you're leaving.

If feelings of doubt are allowed in our lives, we cannot achieve or even conceive of our objectives. Doubt is this inner voice, which often lets us know how incompetent we are. We will eliminate the doubts if we are positive. If we do not, however, questions will continue to dominate our thoughts and make us feel inadequate. Our feelings are right! The thoughts take over, and we assume soon that regardless of what we do, it wouldn't be much, why even bother? Over time we begin to define this mentality, and we disappear into the shadows.

It all begins with an act or action followed by a feeling. When we allow questionable thoughts to dominate our thinking process, many important life changes can be missed. The doubts make for a negative outlook, and the desire to concentrate on good things in our lives is lost. Then the ability to learn and grow is slowed. Many are cynical, depressed, or nervous, and a life of mediocrity with little hope for the future emerges. Now, I'm sure it's not the life that you're hoping for.

Does your self-doubt consume you? Can't you stop the dubious thoughts? Does your ability to achieve interfere? Start to recognize these events and how often they occur. Be more mindful of and write down what the questions mean.

Who triggers self-doubting?

We are born into cultures where we all have to live up to so many demands.

There is a certain stage of development and stages that are expected to reach each one of us from birth. Unless we are deemed underdeveloped or late, we enter the school system and expect to complete primary, elementary, and secondary schools. Our parents have their own expectations of us. Our school teachers expect us. After high school, we are expected to make a career decision and decide where we want to learn this ability; what school we attend what college we want, what job title we want to hold.

Once we are ready to enter the business world, we should demand more and achieve more. Then there is society's expectation, reputation, popularity, and material possessions. Today, our society defines success and accomplishment through its net worth.

The above criteria are required to be met in order to be considered functional or effective in modern society. Children are hardly allowed to run freely with little fear. Rather, they are afraid of making mistakes. We live in an age of high motivation and enthusiasm, and everybody seems successful. Image is an important thing, and some even encourage you to fake it until you make it. Many of you feel pressured to live up to these standards and feel as if you don't let yourself or your family down. So from that very first year, in elementary school, you feel like you are a specimen under the microscope afraid of being harmed and where there is a constant pressure to perform or a fear of refusal.

True, the standards set for us help us to reach high levels of achievement and satisfaction in life. For many, however, this may have the opposite effect. If you have no self-confidence, such social or family expectations can lead to doubt and fear. When you have self-doubt, your shortcomings are compounded to the point of disrupting the thinking process and distorting the belief system.

Some of the following can trigger doubt: believe that your security emotionally depends on something or someone.

Feelings of Low inferiority self-esteem, feeling a lack of control over your life, feeling you are not sufficiently good or knowledgeable to attempt even the smallest tasks.

Predicting failure even before you begin, unresolved psychological trauma, Depression, the Accomplice Doubting itself is a sign of greater fear in an atmosphere that gives rise to doubt and negativity. You know you are afraid, but it's hard to figure out what you are afraid of. It may be fear of failure, anxiety, or even fear of success. The doubts begin to take hold, and the inner critic is eager and willing to help you rationalize your doubts.

Self-awareness is a key step towards overcoming fear and eliminating doubt. Every hope is lost when fear is allowed to dominate. Sadly, we cannot even accept our fears and doubts, but they hold our lives under control. This is why it is important to have mentors, coaches, or staff next to us. The more we know about ourselves, the more we are attuned to what holds us apart. The more aware we are, the more motivated we are to do something about it. We will start to recognize the root of our fears. Is it the way you were born from previous trauma, or is it an insight into the present or the future? Is it a lack of trust? With growing awareness of ourselves, we can accept our doubts more easily and deal with life more productively. Self-consciousness causes affirmation that opens the door to healing. It helps us to seek the help we need to overcome our concerns and to cast doubt.

Were you conscious of your fears? Do you wonder what's holding you back? Take the time to look indoors. Make yourself true. Be real. This is the beginning of the process of doubting. If not, let a mentor or a coach give you the guidance you need to go forward.

Letting go of doubt, we all have moments of doubt in our lives. Others can let go of them and not let them take over, while others are subjected to intrusive ideas that undermine your ability to succeed. And remember that all of them are thoughts. So who's keeping that question in mind? You do! You do! Let's look at how doubts can be released.

The best way to cast doubt would be to build confidence in oneself. It means that you feel better about your own abilities. If you feel incapacitated and begin to doubt yourself, fear awaits you just around the corner to move into your psyche. When anxiety falls into the subconscious, the pessimistic conversation starts, the self-criticism emerges, and the vicious cycle begins. Here are a few ways to establish your confidence.

Educate yourself in whatever you try to achieve. Take a course, participate in seminars, workshops, meet people, and the network. The more you know, the better you feel, and empowerment eliminates doubts.

Join positive people who appreciate your talents and support your efforts. Get reviews on your proposals-it will most certainly be more critical and beneficial. Avoid negative people. Negative people are also full of doubts and will work to bring you down to fear. You will cast further doubt, and your efforts may seem futile.

Set realistic goals. Someone once said, "When you have any questions, take the next step." Realistic measures make sure you are able to do that and develop your confidence. When you set unrealistic goals, you will most likely be short, leading to your self-doubt. When you do every practical job, your confidence will grow, your doubts will diminish, and your self-doubt will be reduced.

Learn how to deal with losses. Throughout life, achievements and failures can occur. Obviously, you want the best result, but when there is frustration, or things don't go as expected, you need to see this in the game of life. Use the reverses to learn and improve the game plan. This is not the time to doubt and challenge your efforts. Get input from a field expert, make the necessary adjustments, and move on.

Join more positive self-talk. Speak to yourself as if you want to make a skeptical friend feel better. Remember, "You can do it." Make positive statements to yourself all day long until it becomes a habit. Such comments tend to replace self-doubt.

Learn how to deal with criticism. In life, people will always try to put you reject or down your efforts. Rejection is an awful thing and can easily be expressed in the form of suspicions into our thinking. I saw customers who earn tremendous gratitude for their efforts, but if someone criticizes them, it ruins all their success. Talk about how illogical it is and don't let others ruin your efforts. Please click here to learn how critique can be handled.

Search for a coach or a mentor. Often, we can't recognize our vicious self-doubt loop. Others could see it, but we couldn't. A coach or mentor will help you discover false values, doubt, and unrealized aspirations that hinder your results. We can also help you determine and overcome the causes of doubt. This form of advice will help you achieve your goals for light-years.

Begin to lose self-doubt today. Look at what frightens you the most and start dealing with them. Don't let your fears govern your life anymore. It's time to look inside and to liberate yourself from doubt so that your full potential is realized.

BRAIN INJURY TRAUMA - 7 WAYS TO IDENTIFY SEVERE HEAD INJURIES

LSD was studied without their knowledge in the late 1950s and the early 1960s by ethical people. These participants started to have weird thoughts and hallucinatory hallucinations. I don't know that these thoughts and dreams arose from the medications they tried, some of them were overwhelmed, and some committed suicides, perhaps because they felt they were insane.

You will know that you've hit your head or been traumatized in your mind, so you might not understand that your brain has been affected. Some symptoms can be present, and you can become very confused about their origin, especially if the head trauma was just mild. The consequence of this uncertainty will harm the well-being of the patient tremendously. It can lead to broken relationships, depression or suicide, and general misfortune. A brain injury must be treated. It may take time to recover, and sometimes the recovery is not complete. The key to maintaining your health, family, and friends is to accept that you have a brain injury.

Three instances of brain injury not immediately noticed.

Vera got her head hit by a lead from the dog that had lost her owner. Vera was taken to the hospital but released the same day and does not recollect the incident. Like most people returning home after a minor head injury, Vera did not realize that there was damage internally with external injuries. Vera's life was not the same over the next few months. She had a sleeping problem. She found it difficult to cope with her demanding job. Her husband felt he stepped on the shells of her egg as he spoke to her. One day the toast stuck into the toaster, and Vera hurled the toaster so violently that it smashed a photo on the other wall. Everything conducts, before a knock on the head, totally out of character for Vera.

Julie is another example, my mom. We traveled along a quiet country road with Julie driving our small Peugeot 305 while meeting a speedy drunk driver who is about 70 mph on our side of the road. Julie made maybe 25 mph so that the eventual impact was extreme. Seeing Julie's mask, the steering column went forward and did very serious damage to her upper and lower jaws. Julie has been in the hospital for months, but the real repair work started when it was published. No short-term memory, mood changes, no tolerance to less, and irrational irritability, to name just a few symptoms.

Paul's been a chronic snorer to noise, and often, his wife slept in the spare room. Once they booked holidays, they booked separate hotel rooms to allow Paul's wife to sleep. Once Paul lost his job, his family found it very hard to get along with him, and he was becoming deeply depressed.

Paul was then convinced to go to his doctor, who prescribed a costly gadget called a CPAP to support Paul at night. Once he went to sleep, he was supposed to wear the mask. What they didn't know at that moment was that Paul's breathing stopped for a long time during the night. This reduced the amount of oxygen in the brain that causes brain injury. Paul was suffering from a brain injury, reportedly.

There are many minor symptoms or indications that show if someone had a brain injury, and I shall describe the seven most prominent ones here.

Sign One. Choose the second instance above. Loss of memory for short while. Our short-run memory deals with the reason why we chat, why we went to the kitchen. In Julie's situation, though she remembered ten years ago stuff, she couldn't remember ten minutes ago stuff. It took years for Julie to achieve an acceptable level of short-term memory. Vera would be a few paragraphs in a chapter and lose the story thread.

Sign two. Irrational irritability. Paul was a factory boss who supervised seven workers while controlling one machine or another's own production. Juggling schedules and always with a positive outlook. He had a mood change after his brain injury by sleep apnea. He would snap on his work and avoid him as much as possible with his young son and daughter. Instead of Paul, they chose to deal with their mother. Since Julie had come out from the hospital and screamed at me for nothing, then five minutes later, she was all laughing. Ten years down the line, the excessive irritability remains only about 10% of its previous ferocity.

Sign Three. Low time of attention. Julie used to have a demanding job with hundreds of vehicles running a fleet. She would have up to 20 questions hanging in the air at once. By the end of the day, everyone would be satisfactorily sorted and satisfied. Over one year, Julie saved half a million pounds in fuel costs by constantly reviewing where and how fuel was bought. Julie can only do one job one time after the crash since she loses control far to fast. She is easily distracted and must be left alone to concentrate on the task.

Sign four. Sign four. Problems of balance. In acute cases, a brain-injured person sometimes feels dizzy and feels that their muscles don't work together. This often leads to problems keeping equilibrium while walking or performing demanding tasks. Julie likes her horse, but her balance is very bad since the incident, and she has fallen off several times because of her inability to balance well enough. Vera fell down the stairs a few days after returning to work. Luckily she wasn't injured, but her talents made her doubt, and she grew sad and depressed.

Sign five. Cognitive power decreased. We take our thinking abilities for granted. When our thought and cognitive capacities are compromised, and we don't know why it is a brain injury, it can lead to depression, suicidal thinking, and the surrender of life. Given that people are able to reason, interpret, and express their feelings, cognitive abilities are very necessary when those powers are that. When Paul returned to work, he discovered that the second nature of operating machinery needed total concentration. Even routine operations required a certain focus, which Paul found hard, although he had hardly had to rethink before.

Sign Six. Loss of self-confidence. The old advice when you fall off a bike is to get back on straight away, so you don't lose trust. Individuals with brain injuries often lose confidence. It's like the bicycle dropped, but they failed to get back on. Vera was only so slightly injured that the hospital didn't keep her overnight. When she went home, Vera felt like she was missing what she was going to do. She felt like the wind was knocked out of her. The sensation was emotional rather than physical. Driving was no problem for Vera before, but she was suddenly concerned about getting behind the wheel. She particularly started to fear the drive at night. Vera never had before thought about it.

Sign Seven. Black moods and depression. Depression Psychologists may demonstrate that a condition can cause depression. Brain chemistry and body chemistry may cause it. A person can grow depressed for many things. Someone with a brain injury is often anxious, almost regularly. Depression can be a result of many factors, but it is also a sign of a brain injury that must always be taken into account.

CHAPTER FOUR

EMOTIONAL AND PHYSICAL TRAUMA – METHODS OF OVERCOMING THEM

Emotional trauma can be just as fragile as physical trauma. The unintended side effect of physical trauma is emotional trauma. Whilst emotional trauma without physical trauma may occur, emotional trauma physically affects us. The trauma's weakening effects are well known. Therefore, it is important to recover from any trauma if a person wants to live a life as safe as possible.

Security is the most important ingredient in recovery from any trauma. It must ensure that safe people are a must in safe places. The best are those trained to listen, be unjustified, and feel empathic. My understanding is that most of these individuals are psychologists and mental counselors. Continuing work supports thinking about a trauma experience with another person as the best way to recover from trauma. Tell the story as many times as necessary to extract from you the burden of full responsibility, try to make sense of the trauma, and incorporate the experience into our own understanding. The traumatic experience can also be experienced at different levels, including at the somatic and visual levels.

Having a therapist/counselor with whom you feel safe is a challenge — some posts on finding a good therapist and what good therapy is written. A good therapist doesn't make a person dysfunctional but perceives a client as greater than his / her issues. A good therapist also understands that a person must manage his / her issues if he/she shows frustration and learn to cope with and express that anger safely. A good therapist won't call a client a "fearful person."

Great therapists also know how to inspire their clients, and many people have changed and become healthier. A good therapist knows his own skills, is sensitive, caring, imaginative, and reliable. There is a spirit of cooperation in good therapy, and the interaction between the therapist and the client is important. Good therapy is both verbal and cognitive, using emotional and cognitive strategies that allow a person to heal emotionally and holistically. A good therapist can also refer a client to another therapist if it is the customer's best judgment.

Working in a group is another powerful way to heal traumatic experiences. At a party, a consumer may find out that many people have similar problems. The benefit is to listen to various Strategies that benefited various people. Although helping organizations are excellent for this form of treatment, therapeutic groups can be better. A support group consists of people with similar problems and often has no qualified leader. A counseling group is also composed of people with similar problems, but the group phase is guided by a trained therapist. Training is an important part of trauma rehabilitation. Therapists have been trained and often use research-based methods, such as Dialectic Behavioral Therapy, to promote group work.

Sometimes a person works on a trauma they are conscious of, and underneath it has reminders of other trauma. Sometimes our unresolved unconscious memories of our early childhood contribute to similar situations being recreated in an attempt to solve early childhood trauma. Our implicit memory is hard to create a "self-accomplishing prophecy." As a person is working on a current trauma, he or she will also focus on previous trauma.

It is important for people to examine the type of therapy that they want to use. The use of expressive therapies is supported recently by research. Expressive therapies include the recognition and validation of trauma emotions. Emotions involve a number of processes that are essential for the mind. Cognitions and feelings work together. They work together. They can't be separated. Emotions connect with people. Unfortunately, in the first three years of their lives, many people did not experience a healthy relationship, which often leads to people unable to be aware of their feelings. It is important to be aware of our feelings; they also provide us with important information. Trauma may cause people to anesthetize their feelings. Such attempts often take the form of addiction. Many times a person simply sees himself as having no feelings or as being "not emotional." Expressive therapy can be extremely helpful for both these individuals and for those who are more mindful of their feelings.

A cognitive and verbal mix of interventions is often the best. Expressive therapy can produce relatively easy emotions. Cognitive therapy can be used to teach cognitive coping skills. Conduct is a product of thoughts and feelings. Competencies should improve as the emotional and cognitive health of the person improves. A trait of good therapy is the therapist's ability to meet a client, "where he is." The extremely intellectualized client would be an example of this. A good therapist begins with a lot of educational and cognitive training as he incorporates emotional and verbal work.

SPIRITUAL ENERGY, TRAUMA AND THE BODY MIND

Many, if not most of us, have been affected in some form by trauma. Any event or series of events, real or imagined, which triggers the body's mentally bad distress and which the person sees is unable to avoid or track, can be traumatic. The consequences of a single trauma or sequence of traumas and their recovery depend on many factors, including karma, both for the soul and the body.

Although historically, we consider trauma like physical or serious traumatic events such as wars or disasters, the psychological community has recognized that frequent declines or other unsuitable encounters can have a profound effect on the psyche. The values we have learned from our families also serve as a model of affection for our future relationships. Medical problems and increasingly invasive methods will easily add to life's trauma reservoir. The social stress and peer pressure, particularly in the sexual arena, all contribute to the warehouse in which we live.

We have two conflicting karmic tracks: the soul that lives in one lifespan and has many incarnations, and the body that has a genetic history across successive generations. We each bear the implicit burden of trauma, remorse, and patterns of attraction. When tandem with the present traumatic experience, this can be an unbearable responsibility. The soul's karma is psychologically contained in consciousness, which influences the physicality of that manifestation, where and when we are embodied. The body is energized into the multiple layers of the body-mind, which then can affect consciousness.

We have different acupuncture meridians that are more fragile than others, depending on our genetic heritage. The method of acupuncture is in the esthetic or esthetic body. When there is an energetic/emotional impact on the body's mind, the meridian(s) are affected and begin to decline at some point, which can result in pain in their respective organs or system.

Some of those with memories of sexual abuse seem to have embraced the fantasies and guilty ideas of the adults they were exposed to. Children are very responsive mentally, so reading the minds of those around them is not unusual. Perhaps people with obsessive compulsive behaviors are trying to protect themselves from other people's intrusive thinking. It doesn't matter to the human consciousness if it was a real event or if it is taken from another, but it is nevertheless real.

Patterns of dysfunction can be genetically inherited for many generations. Disable energetic encoding, and the pattern can be broken more quickly. Moms traumatized themselves also hold the energy in their solar plexus, which can imprint on the fetus. Sperm can also bear the father's energetic as well as genetic residue at conception. If trauma is unsolved, this imprint can be inserted into the sperm that leads to the offspring. Obviously, there is the whole cycle of parental suffering in which to succeed.

For many people, particularly those whose suffering was due to human actions, guilt and shame also add up to the strain. Sexually abused children or young adults often have the embarrassment of the positive reaction of the body to the violence as well as shame that arises from different misunderstandings. The perpetrators of tragic events like the Holocaust are guilty of any perceived misdeeds committed both for survival and the simple fact of having survived.

Naturally, every person will respond to a certain stimulus differently, and that which is slumped by one can become a deep wound in another. After a lightning strike, what makes one tree prosper and another falter and die? The factors involved are more than the stars that are visible in the sky, and nobody can really predict the result.

The list of symptoms shown by people due to trauma is quite different. They are responsible for the range of human dysfunction, including the original wound. In many situations, an energy boost is analogous to an electric condenser that releases an extreme pressure to overcome inertia. Whenever the trigger is triggered, an overwhelming energy release threatens to consume the human. This can turn the treatment into a potentially volatile task.

Psychologists and spiritual / energy healers have taken tremendous strides in several decades to recognize and to establish effective tools for coping with trauma. Various modes use sensor switches, such as quick eye motion and taping to disperse trigger mechanisms. Some are actively working on letting the energy run out while others are seeking to disseminate the Karmic debt, reducing the level of conscious culpability dramatically. Soul healing is being used in many situations to put together the broken portions of the individual, and the growing popularity of 12-step programs has helped others escape the misery of drug abuse, promoting exposure to underlying diseases.

Regardless of the specific course of action or variations that arise following trauma, rehabilitation involves courage and determination by the customer/patient and a strong commitment to healing. It also needs the therapist to have a high level of expertise and experience. In any case, the growing recognition of these problems and increasingly successful coping strategies offer hope for those who have historically been stuck in their past experiences.

Trauma is something most of us will have to deal with on our life journey at some point. Yes, it is projected that sometimes 50% to 90% of us will have to deal with it.

Psychological trauma is always a product of an experience that overwhelms the victim and does not handle or fully control the emotions produced by that experience.

The subconscious mind is disturbed by distress by an incident or a number of events, and this has profoundly affected the individual's functioning.

Essential and effective though it is certainly for the traumatized individual, the actual experience itself is less essential on a psychological level than its interpretation and reaction.

It explains why one person can very well shrug a similar event off but creates real difficulties in another. What can be a traumatic experience is not traumatic for one person.

Trauma itself can happen on a life journey at any time.

This can occur during infancy, and as a result of, for example, psychological, physical abuse, or extreme poverty and can leave the child traumatized in adulthood.

And traumas arise later in life, triggered by neglect, injuries, injury, crime, war, death, and natural disaster.

Although trauma itself is painful, about 8% are more debilitating and paralyzing effects of the Post Traumatic Stress Disorder (PTSD) trauma.

If left untreated, PTSD can have serious consequences for the patient, serious implications, and ability to function at work or interpersonal level.

PTSD also stems from real physical damage encounters or experiences. Occasionally, however, psychological and emotional distress may cause it where no actual physical harm is involved.

Very often, though, it blends both aspects.

While a persistent and significant emotional response to trauma is essentially post-traumatic stress disorder, it differs from combat stress or traumatic stress in that it is typically much more severe and not at all transitory.

PTSD has also historically been identified as shell shock, combat tiredness, and post-traumatic stress syndrome.

Yet fighting is not sufficient to be affected by PTSD, any real trauma to the nervous system—such as a car accident or death, addiction to drugs or sexual assault—can lead to it.

However, whatever the cause, the resulting symptoms of trauma are real and distressing for a person who has to experience them.

Those with this type of trauma can experience chronic and acute anxiety, frustration, sleep disturbance, disturbing thoughts, breathtaking disorder, or nightmares. We also find it very difficult to think about trauma cases.

We find it difficult or impossible to effectively deal with and incorporate these issues on the subconscious level of the mind, owing to their upsetting nature.

And here, transformational hypnotherapy with experience can be extremely useful, offering psychological care that can lead to a full recovery from trauma.

The unconscious mind, working with a skilled and highly trained transformational hypnotherapist, can be guided to reconstitute traumatic experiences of the past in order to neutralize and reverse the damage.

The truth is that the person survived, given the frightening expectations and beliefs that were instilled during the traumatic experience. Ultimately, he or she did it through.

The details of the traumatic experience exist with the right trauma therapy, but the meaning and psychological symptoms previously induced by these facts have always been changed.

Effective trauma care allows the patient to deal with what happened so that the person can then let his or her life go and go on.

For example, leaving the traumatized person in no way means that he has to forget what has happened in the past.

Nonetheless, it very often means that an abuser or any person who has actively participated in the traumatic experience must be encouraged to forgive.

It's not for religious reasons nor is it altruistic in any way. It's simply because failure to do so holds the person in contact with the past, retains and supports the harm the ongoing trauma pain, the continuing emotional and mental trauma.

It must be stressed that the traumatized person is encouraged to forgive. It is not necessarily the person or people who may have caused the trauma. In reality, the person or persons responsible for this very often do not know forgiveness.

But the traumatized person is released and released through real forgiveness. The patient is shown how to forgive the past with the help of transformational hypnotherapy so as to heal and move on with their lives.

If you or someone you care about has the truly debilitating and deteriorating consequences of trauma, it can really be done.

Operating with a well-qualified, skilled transition hypnotherapist, you will put the trauma behind you and continue with life.

With the right kind of support, you can truly recover from trauma and liberate yourself from past experiences.

CHAPTER FIVE

HEAD TRAUMA AND BRAIN INJURY - LEARN WHAT TO DO BEFORE IT HAPPENS

It might be a motorcycle accident or even a car crash. Or hit by an object suddenly. Perhaps someone performed an assault. Or it might come from being too close to a blast that causes the head to change suddenly. Traumatic brain injury happens far too often, however. It is estimated that approximately 1.7 million occurrences occur in the United States. Therefore, it may impact you, either directly or indirectly. (i)The fact is that the harm could be severe even if nothing is outwardly wrong. That is why it helps to have certain facts at hand to determine how bad it may be. Whether mild or fatal, the bottom line is that getting the right help means quicker and more complete recovery as quickly as possible.

How do you take the place of brain trauma?

The egg analogy can give you an idea of how severe brain damage can occur without any sign of damage or even any external damage. Think of the cranium, which houses the brain, like an egg's shell with the brain like a yolk in the egg. The outer cranium/shaft may remain intact when traumatized, but inside the brain/egg yolk may be violently pushed when thrown into the white of the egg or cerebral spinal fluid.

What should you do straight away

Don't move your head because you can have a broken neck and cause them to stop breathing or to be paralyzed. If you've got something cold, then just place it next to your head with your face.

Instead, if it is someone who is injured and not you, you will make a great difference by letting emergency workers know the extent of the injury before they even arrive at the scene. Research has shown that the quicker an injured person is evaluated and the more emergency treatment appropriate, the better the result along the way.

Here is some of what they'll want to know when you talk to an emergency person on the cell phone before they arrive. Besides whether the person breathes, it allows them to know: the eye opens the reaction of the individual: open your eyes spontaneously, blink, respond to verbal stimulus, order or speech with your eyes, only pain, or no answer.

How do you react to verbal input: do you appear oriented? Confused in their conversation, even if they are able to answer questions, do they respond inadequately or with unintended speech, or do they not answer?

What's your engine response? Should they follow movement commands (e.g. raise your finger, stick your tongue, etc.). Acting cautiously in response to pain, removing pain, flexing in response to the pain, or stretching the body in response to pain, or not responding?

The answers to these questions can be that doctors may say where part of the brain can be damaged, the extent and severity of the attack, and the degree of damage, for example, and if the person's head injury is mild, moderate, or serious. [ii] The consequences of a traumatic brain injury, the individual may have been released after the incident is treated and medically stable. Furthermore, this does not mean that traumatic brain injuries are induced. The signs and signs of a TBI may "even be missed, as people may look okay even though they act or feel different. Some common signs and symptoms are that brain injury is traumatic and remains a problem: headaches or pain in the neck that does not leave; difficulties Targeted dietary care, massage and/or chiropractic therapies, supplements, physical therapy, or homeopathy can be used.

Because judgment and decision-making are compromised in the accident, others may need to play an active role in ensuring that such treatment options are established and instigated. The very consequences of the injury will play against the injured person who can find certain choices, schedule their appointments, and continue to appear for them.

The bottom line is that the faster these are introduced, the more likely the person will recover fully.

BRAIN TRAUMA INDUCES DEPRESSION

Over two percent of the U.S. population has reported traumatic brain injury, with around 25-50 percent of the survivors experiencing a certain degree of depression within one year of injury. When a person is depressed, he or she is stuck in a boring mood and feels like no escape. Nevertheless, the suffering caused by the incarceration of post-traumatic brain injury disorder can be alleviated by interventions.

Injuries of the post-traumatic brain tend to cause instability, panic, intense depression, dejection, and hopelessness in survivors. Many people are affected for a short period of time and others for a longer period of time. Temporary depression lasts up to three months and it is a depressive condition without anxiety. Long-term depression lasts about six months and it is followed by anxiety.

Influences

Because TBI is often depressed and is followed by psychosocial dysfunction after brain injury, researchers believe that TBI and depression are associated. As a report by Lehr, "so-called endogenous signs of TBI" are directly associated with damaged brain tissue contributing to changes in behavior.

Such direct effects of brain wounds often include changes in behavior and social emotions such as can inadequacy, aggressiveness, or regular mood changes. Some of the psychological impairments may include deficiencies in self-confidence, self-regulation, self-esteem, fluency in the expression of thinking and feeling, the ability to interpret feelings, and other people's subtle nonverbal signals, and the ability to undertake tasks or functions in relation. Any such psychosocial disorders can lead to depression. Depression is common due to such uncontrollable and abrupt changes in one's life. Patients after injury, for example, are often unable to express their ideas and emotions clearly. We become segregated by being uncommunicative, which can result in soreness, anger, and, eventually, depression. Neurological and/or cognitive deficits are often interrelated with emotional difficulties. Brain dysfunction affects the thinking, judgment, personal relationships, and perspective of a person. Jimmy, a teenager who has been damaged in the closed head, has a symptom rash; he can be used as an example. He has difficulty reading the feelings of others and sometimes misunderstands the underlying meaning of what he is told. He already tends to get rid of others and deficits like this distancing him from his friends and family.

The family of Jimmy will support his need to spend time alone, but be mindful that social isolation is one of the most debilitating and upsetting consequences of TBI. Emotional trauma is difficult to read for more information about cloaked chronic disease and pain. We cannot assume that one symptom leads to another, so many affect a survivor transition. The trauma itself or simply, a neurological intervention can only lead to a depressive state; the resulting complications are also present.

Many Factors of Depression

Depression has many factors or causes and is evident in many types of behavior. Feeling depressed is not always easy to detect–a camouflaged illness of varying symptoms. Symptoms were divided into two groups, psychological and vegetative, in a study conducted by Jorge and his associates. The more serious category of depressive, psychological symptoms consists of anxiety, brooding, loss of interest, hopelessness, intentions for suicide, social disengagement, self-depreciation, lack of self-confidence, basic reference ideas, guilty reference ideas, pathological culpability, and irritability. Vegetative signs include more severe depression, autonomous anxiety, nervous foreboding, morning depression, weight loss or gain, the lateness of sleep, subjective energy, early morning awakening. It was noted that some patients with TBI could deny the existence of depressed mood as part of general unconsciousness or denial. Brain damage leads to psychological and social issues. Symptoms such as these can result in a depressive disorder or cause it.

Modifying depression

In addition to medical interventions (e.g., antidepressants, mood stabilizers, etc.), physical, mental, or psychosocial operations may change the depressed condition. The use of therapeutic approaches is an example of a physical solution to interfere in a depressing situation. Emotional recovery can be accomplished through engaging in activities such as the performing arts; psychosocial healing can occur by involvement in support groups for brain injury. Some or all of these approaches may be used for brain injury survivors, and support, motivation, and participation of peers and families is important.

Emotional Rehabilitation

The arts will help reduce the overall burden of an individual and allow him or her to build a deficit benefit. Emotional therapy is the expressive arts can be used in recovery to help the person with TBI release energy and understand themselves.

Painting and dance are two creative methods that can lead to self-understanding, emotional self-expression and stress minimized (i.e., many other artistic methods can be used to enable a student to deal with distress and personal changes)

Poetry

Writing poetry is a literary device that allows a survivor to be remembered, articulated and embraced. It is a special recovery technique for brain damage because it. This poem about depression, "Melt Down," comes from a chapter on brain injury symptoms.

Painting

Expression by painting enables feelings and behaviors to be consciously or symbolically conveyed. Exaggeration or focus on specific sections of a painting may convey the strength of feeling. Certain distortions, such as versatile color use and shape exaggeration, can also and should be promoted to improve the emotional impact of painting. The painting often serves as a reminder for a person, and therefore the painting act will help to familiarize him with his emotions of the present or the past and to make difficult memories contact, redefine or heal.

Dance.

Dance is an expression of emotion and imagination. It helps to learn how the person moves, how other people perceive their body language, and how to develop their own form of self-expression. It can also be used as an act of seeking freedom by vocal gestures (Talbott, M., 1996). Dance may help alleviate the effect of stress in life and also exercise some brain processes that may have been affected by a brain injury. The roles of dance include the mechanisms that regulate equilibrium, coordination, motion, and the synchronization of thought and action of the cerebellum, basal ganglia, and Pons.

Creative compensation is an autonomous adaptation mechanism. A survivor can use this inspiration to respond in new and innovative ways to psychosocial or other problems. Susie, a survivor of the TBI, found in the dance course that certain gestures made people smile, even laugh. Susie is a woman who is usually very self-aware when people notice her issues. The next time her slanting news and oblivion attracted the attention of a group of people, Susie grabbed her hand as if she were singing in the air and turned around. Five puzzled spectators ' expressions turned to laughter. It removed Susie from the burden of all and became her imaginative way to compensate.

Psychosocial Recovery

Support groups for patients and their families are strongly recommended. Survivors and their families can provide supporting groups with an atmosphere where each participant can be heard and supported. Families can also find the information they need in meetings. The support group offers peer relationships, input, modeling, and an environment for the person who has suffered an accident to establish forms of compensation. This allows a person to use modeling of others with the same problems, to feel less alone, to show skills, and to support others, increasing their self-esteem. The workshops can also help people develop communication and social skills and raise awareness of injury-related deficiencies and residual properties.

The behavior of partners, relatives, friends, teachers, and associates can greatly affect a person with post-traumatic depression. Many points of view tend to deter the recovery of the victim (i.e., a defensive attitude may prevent a person from participating in activities that may be necessary for the patient to get around). It is important not to speak to a distressed person with a feeling that he needs to relieve him of his or her life's troubles; better approach an inspiring survivor, "You're more than your injury." A victim can always take advice and suggestions from friends, family, or therapists; however, healed people can learn to adopt methods to release them from incarceration.

A victim of a brain injury said while preparing for special education for survivors of a brain injury. She studied the correlation between head trauma and depression on the Internet and found only a trace of research, but she knew personally that there was a direct connection. She regards this as "neurological traffic" and considers it possible to redirect bundled nerves and reduce depressive congestion with an awakening effort to replace or supplement medicines. Research in the field is still under progress; the "internal view" of brain injury must be understood.

THE STRUCTURE AND FUNCTION OF THE BRAIN IN RELATING TO THE TRAUMA

The first step in fully understanding the devastating effects of trauma should be a psychological one, namely, to consider the structure and function of the brain that the patient has to use and manage. As an organism, it is the nucleus of its existence and the most complex structure.

The human brain is by far the most complex structure in the universe. "Not even the most advanced computers can match their performance in performing data processing functions. And there's no computer like a sense of self. But each one has a diversified sense of self as a unique individual. "By understanding and processing information about the world within the body and the world outside, it can be considered to be the command enters the nervous system, making it possible for the user to make decisions and to produce changes that ensure physical health and stability in his / her muscles, normally and automatically. Early-life stress causes an increase in the blood stress hormone cortisol and decreases in the number of cortisol receptors in the brain.

Such modifications are thought to predispose anxiety and depression in adulthood when tension and misfortune happen. "Although the majority of brain control mechanisms stop with puberty, two significant developments continue:

(1). Key functional areas of the brain cortex are still adult, but gradually, and

(2). Situated on the threshold of adult life with its expectations and requirements, the person acquires complex cognitive and motor skills.

The era from about 25 to older years can be known as the middle years when up to 30% of the brain's volume can be decreased due to the size of the nerve cell joints that are no longer needed. While this results in subtle behavioral and cognitive changes that intensify in late years, early life intellectual and motor skills have become largely automatic; a person can, therefore, be both functional and alert. This mental and physical activity will delay further by maintaining original and sometimes even new nerve cell connections. Even in the absence of any neurodegenerative disease, the decrease in neuronal, synaptic, and neurotransmitter levels may reduce brain weight, reduce mental flexibility and psychomotor speed, impair the learning of new skills, and reduce processing and responsiveness at significantly advanced ages. Because not all brains age at the same rate, and since physical and mental activity and genetics can affect them positively, declines will vary significantly while long term memory and personality remain.

THE SKULL

Because of the fluid nature of the brain and fragile tissue, the skull is primarily covered by bones.

THE CEREBRAL HEMISPHERES

When seen above, it is apparent that the brain becomes subdivided into two (left and right) cerebral hemispheres that regulate the motor control and senses of the brain. The brain is created by a skull base that includes an occipital, sphenoid, petrous, and frontal bones, creating three bowl-shaped depressions into which the lower parts of the brain are sloping. The activities of the left hemisphere include motor movements on the right side of the body, movement of the two eyes on the right side, touch and discomfort on the right side of the body, and goal-driven preparation. The right hemisphere functions include motor control of the left side of the body, perception of pleasure and discomfort on the left side of the body, eye movement to the left, enjoyment of music and expression in emotional aspects, and rationalization of mental decisions. Two language areas, Broca's area and the Wernicke's area (named after neurologists) are only located in the left hemisphere, although studies have shown that the right hemisphere is the dominant left-winger. Spatial perception is largely in the right hemisphere of everything. The corpus callosum, an array of 250 to 300 million axons, makes connections and contact between the two hemispheres simpler.

A VERTICAL BRAIN PROFILE

When the brain as seen from the side, consist of the upper portion would be the cerebral cortex, the midbrain in the upper part, which stimulates the brain and the emotions, and the brain stem itself, which descends from the thalamus to spinal cord.

THE CEREBRAL

Cortex The forebrain, which is its largest part, is divided into four lobes of the front, parietal, temporal, and occipital cortex. The insular is under the lobes themselves and deep inside the heart. One-third of all nerve cells, or approximately9,000 billion, facilitates neural processing and high levels of executive work, with further functional subdivisions for aspects such as motor control, sound, smell, taste, sight, spatial perception, balance, and planning.

THE BRAIN CORE

A brain nucleus is a group of structures and cells linked to promoting a smooth movement that enhances sensory, endocrine, cognitive, and movement functions. We include the following.

(1). Basal Ganglia: The group of the nerve cells, the basal ganglia, facilitates emotion, decision making, and regulation of movement.

2). Thalamus: Comprising two large, egg-shaped structures, located on either side of the third ventricle, that make up the diencephalon, receiving and interpreting incoming stimuli and information, processing it, and routes or relaying it to or above the brain cortex or below.

3). Hypothalamus: The relatively small hypothalamus is situated just below the thalamus, and controls automatic functions of the nervous system, the glands in the endocrine system, the heart rate and the blood pressures. It also provides conscious fulfillment of animal needs, including food, nutrition, and the internal atmosphere of the body.

THE BRAIN STEM

The brain stem is divided into three components of the midbrain, Pons, and medulla oblongata between thalamus and the spinal cord, and in effect provides three key functions.

(1). It functions as the central nervous system's nervous pathways, which are both up and down bidirectional.

2). As the sensory information processing center, it controls the physical function of an organ through mostly subconscious commands.

3). It helps us to process cranial nervous, sensory information and monitor the muscles and glands of the head and neck for food consumption and digestion and contact through speech and facial expression" The brain stem, which has changed little over the centuries and is almost identical with that of lower foodstuffs, eventually evolved into higher areas, in particular, the cerebral cortex. Its nerve pathways connect it to the spinal cord via the intermediate brainstem.

"The road to the cortex of the brain allows the Amygdala to control movements to fulfill the basic drives and attach objects (such as) snake perception and appropriate emotional responses (such as) fear... "The direction of the hypothalamus stimulates the amygdala to cause changes in physical, emotional responses."

BRAIN CELLS

Nerve cells control brain and spinal cord impulses, feelings and actions.

Nerve cells, also known as neurons, include the data processing and transmission of it to the other nerve cells of that complex brain system. Nerve cells themselves consist of an axon that transmits data to other neurons, tree-like dendrites that stretch to 0.2 inches of information and axon-surfaced sheaths that efficiently and rapidly increase the strength of the electric impulses. Neurotransmitters are chemical messenger molecules which bridge the synaptic interruption between them, cause changes in cell electrical activity and create neuropathy. The transmission rate depends on the diameter of the axon and whether or not the surface is coated with myelin.

The actual transmission of the electrical signal is known as "action potential" and is considered to be an all or no-all-sequence, which means that the interaction is complete or not initiated. In the middle of the break there is no turning back.

Many nerve cell contacts are known to be circuits. Your repeated use as a neuropathy slowly builds stronger bonds, and a person's views are modified to build new ideas with considerable effort.

SYSTEM

Several pathways to activate and respond to brain impulses facilitate physiological, emotional, and behavioral changes, maintain domestic homeostasis and regulation and increase the potential for human survival.

The primary nervous system consists of the brain, the backbone, and the peripheral nervous system (PNS), and is divided into CNS. Sub-nervous system, which regulates voluntary processes and the automatic nervous system, can be further divided.

The limbic system located on the edge of the forebrain (or the "limbus" in Latin), consists of an amygdala; a latin amygdala system, the temporal lobe and the hippocampus, the cortical tissue and the out-flow of amygdala, which links the paper circles to create a link between memory and emotions.

The amygdala itself is essential for the understanding of trauma function and transmission.

"The amygdala's key work is to combine sensory stimulation and emotional experience." This helps us to understand whether they are positive or negative and have a profound significance in influencing future behaviors.

The final system is the autonomic one, so designated because it is considered automatic or not under the conscious control of the person. Subdivided into the sympathetic and parasympathetic nervous systems, they maintain the body's internal environment and use energy reserves during emergency times. Preparing a person for survival-intended actions, the first of the two increases the heart rate, open the airways and redirects blood from the stomach to the muscles. The second both complements and counteracts the first by restoring regulation, thus lowering the heart rate and decreasing blood pressure. Full simultaneous activation of both divisions seldom occurs. The enteric system, also an autonomic system division, controls the movement of digested substances, food, and liquid through the gastrointestinal tract.

CHEMICALS AND HORMONES

Several chemicals and hormones are instrumental in behavior and emotion.

Adrenalin, both a hormone and a neurotransmitter, is released into the bloodstream during stressful, emergency, and life-threatening times, whether they are real or only perceived, to create fight-or-flight responses intended to improve and increase a person's safety and survival-that is, it increases the heart rate, blood pressure, airflow to the lungs, and blood flow to the muscles. During panic attacks, it acts like an overheating engine, overriding the autonomic system and rendering it impossible for the person to regulate himself. Cortisol, a stress hormone secreted by the adrenal cortex, controls mood, motivation, and fear, and aids in the body's fight-or-flight responses. Dopamine is a neurotransmitter chemical used by the neurons of the midbrain's substantia nigra to regulate the motor activity, pathway-routed to the limbic system, and medial cortex to augment motivation and cognition. Although it rewards behavior by amplifying the brain's pleasure centers, misuse of its pathway can lead to addiction. Melatonin is a hormone produced by the pineal gland to control circadian rhythms, a 24-hour cycle in the physiological processes of living beings. Finally, serotonin is a neurotransmitter used by brainstem cells to control sleep-wake cycles, moods, and pain perceptions by means of upper and lower pathways.

PART 2: TRAUMA

Familiarization with brain structure and function can immeasurably aid the neurological understanding of trauma, which alerts a person to perceived or possible danger by gearing the body for survival-promoting strategies. There are levels of trauma severity, however. Major ones include life-threatening accidents, rapes, losses, abuse, parental or primary caregiver alcoholism, Para-alcoholism, and/or abandonment, and horrific events, such as wars, terrorism, the 9/11 attacks, and the holocaust. Lesser traumas include living with someone who himself suffers from post-traumatic stress disorder (PTSD); overexposure to media reports about terrorism; growing up with economic insecurity; harassment, sexual or otherwise, in school or in the workplace; extended periods of illness or pain; and behaving in ways that are opposed to the person's core beliefs. Integral to all of these adverse experiences is fear. "Fear is the acute emotion that is usually experienced when confronted with a dangerous or painful situation, whereas anxiety is the anticipation of painful and unpleasant experiences and maybe felt over a much longer period of time". Incoming stimuli, which can be numbered in the hundreds of thousands on any given day, enter the brain through the thalamus, its router, which then relays it through two possible paths-the slow upper one or the faster lower one. In the case of the slow upper route, information entering and routed by the thalamus is sent to the cerebral cortex for processing and understanding, and the hippocampus. In the case of the fast lower route, the information is sent directly to the amygdala. This pathway, sparking the characteristic overtaking and controlling sensations because the amygdala is inextricably tied to the hypothalamus, results in several fundamental differences:

1). It is faster, overriding the logic and reasoning of the upper route through the cerebral cortex, whose path it cuts off.

2). It floods the blood with adrenalin stress hormones, which increase the heart and blood pressure rates.

3). It activates the sympathetic division of the autonomic nervous system, which increases airflow to the lungs and redirects blood to the muscles, initiating the survival-promoting, fight-or-flight response.

4). It drives the person's response behavior, controlling him with floods of stress hormones to either combat or flees from the danger, real or perceived.

5). It is reactive in nature.

6). It creates, via the sympathetic division, a rupture in the autonomic system, which the parasympathetic division cannot counteract or reregulate, leaving the energy locked in. Because it cannot be discharged, later retriggering create post-traumatic stress disorder. Like emotionally going offline, the person who suffers from PTSD can have any or all of the following symptoms: bracing, exaggerated startle effects, eruptive rage as opposed to anger, hypervigilance, numbing, dissociation, cognitive distortions and misinterpretations, the inability to sustain intervals of calm without assistance, and the same emotional and physiological effects that were generated by the original trauma, leaving him to believe that it is just as real now as it was then. Understanding these neurological, physiological, and emotional concepts can greatly aid an adult child, who experienced abusive, dysfunctional, and alcoholic upbringings, in his life's plight. Most likely subjected to an original trauma at an early age that could be measured in months, unable to resolve or even understand it, hyper vigilant for repeated danger as he is held captive to sometimes raging, out-of-control parents or primary caregivers, developing PTSD, and adding layer upon layer to his dilemma, he is forced to filter much of his life through the amygdala, leaving little surprise as to why he was (or still is) afraid of people, places, and things.

CHAPTER SIX

THE TRIBRAIN AND TRAUMA THERAPY

If someone has a trauma, they are immediately shocked. This resembles hypnosis very much. In the case of hypnosis, a person is more suggestible and appears to recall everything that took place in this setting, even if it is subconscious. This is why a person, when abused, clearly remembers what he felt like a victim and also remembers what he or she was about being an abuser.

If an incident is stressful and upsetting enough, we prefer to internalize it in an unhealthy attempt to control or manage it. In some cases, the survivor unconsciously assumes the role of the perpetrators and appears to be attracted to offenders and he is sorry for them. Some take on the role of victims and then prey on others. Some people do something about both.

That propensity is the basis of Freud's desire to repeat. It is a misguided effort to understand the definition. If we can't handle a job, we become obsessed with the task, before we figure out what we did wrong and solve the problem. The idea of mastery is one of the main ways people learn.

But a repetition compulsion is simply repeatedly doing the same thing. The abused person also feels guilty of abuse and therefore chooses perpetrators unconsciously even when they try to pick a nice and safe person. This is healthy learning.

The mechanisms of the trauma and post-traumatic stress disorder need to be understood by the three minds as well as the body. The brain and the cortex are the human part of the brain and work through rational thinking. This brain is jutted causal and linear. Therefore you will follow the directions voluntarily when something explained to that part of the brain, and the individual agrees. It is our brain's conscious part. That is the part of our brain that is aimed at traditional psychotherapy or speech therapy. The Limbic organ is an older brain that resembles the brains of all mammals. It consists primarily of chemicals called neurotransmitters, which help us to think and feel.

Medulla Oblongata is the third brain and is found at the base of the skull. It's a brain that we share with every reptile. This discusses impulses and mechanisms that are unconscious. This sure isn't logical as she thinks.

All the cells in the body are related and able to remember the body and are, therefore, all minute brains. Candice Pert, the Endorphin System discoverer, pretends that our emotions must be somewhat recognized by the Enkephalin system in every cell of our body. She claims this network of endorphins/feelings is a very advanced but complex brain system. Every cell consists of a real sense of a primary primitive brain. Such brains also work faster than the others I mentioned.

All the brains, except the human brain, are based on the dog or conditioning of Pavlov. If something is sufficiently repeated or so powerful that learning is impressed, it is extremely difficult to dislodge it even when situations change.

That's why emotions or patterns so slowly change after the unconscious thoughts have shifted. Without any kind of intervention to change or block the dynamic stimulation/response, the earlier brains and the body often lie 2-5 years behind the brain and sometimes remain actively active indefinitely. That is why it is so difficult for people to improve and often confused and frustrated by their failure to do so. This can make people very intelligent unable to solve a problem, and therefore believe that they must be stupid or faint-hearted. This isn't the case.

There are three main ways to change quicker and less slowly than traditional psychotherapy, which mostly only deals with the human brain.

Hypnosis is the first technique. Because people under hypnosis are more reactive and suggestible, this is often a successful way to decrease stimulus/response patterns. A clinician should ask the customer to experience the past painful experience more peacefully or effectively than he had as a child. This changes the experience of the original trauma. Hypnosis may be very helpful, but it does not seem as helpful as some of the newer methods mentioned below. It seems that modern therapy models also yield more congruence and a longer-lasting improvement than with hypnosis. It's also longer and less flexible.

Furthermore, EMDR is an effective and fast way of dealing with and treating trauma. It is a modern, fast, and relatively painless therapy. It is based on theory which REM or fast eye movements occurring during dreaming transform short-term memory to long-term memory. Long-term memory is not related to too much feeling or immediacy. Clients find the trauma's most impressive feature while the therapist pushes a few fingers of his hand in front of his face to trigger quick eye movements. It looks like recreating the pain and inducing a little abreaction. Generally, after a few sessions, customers say that they recall the pain without emotion.

The third and fourth methods are herbal therapy, but the Neuro Emotional Technique or NET(TM) is by far more advanced, more flexible, and more efficient. Initially, chiropractors practiced neuro-emotional techniques(TM) or NET(TM) and only later taught them, mental health therapists. It's still very difficult to find a professional counselor in this method. This draws on Chinese medicine and acupuncture and meridians. It enables a clinician to track the current traumas and emotions of the body and see if these emotions are related to previous traumas. It then helps a clinician to gently touch a few points of the body around the spinal cord and removes toxic memory. It helps the affected individual, in today's adult style, to be more fully involved in effective action and change. If the feelings of abandonment of an adult are compounded by getting the feelings of abandonment when they are ten years old, an individual is less competent. NET(TM) quickly and effectively removes old and current traumas remaining in the body.

TFT is another simple and painless therapy, or Thought Field Therapy, also based on the Meridian System, and this method is being trained by more practitioners. This is not as versatile as NET(TM), and I believe that its diagnostic capability is limited, but it relieves some fears and phobias by touching on different acupressure points quite effectively.

All these "power treatments" seem to alter other layers than the conscious plane. Often they are faster and more efficient than traditional therapy. This is because they concentrate on the more fragile brains that are not normally accessed through older models of therapy. I fully believe that understanding is necessary and that conventional therapy sometimes provides it, but progress is not as simple or total without access to the basic brains. The current treatments do this most effectively.

TRAUMA AND TRAUMATIC STRESS

A young mother took a doctor to a seven-year-old. Suddenly, the young man, an intelligent boy, began to throw himself into the school. He asked his mother not to send him to school. While researching, we found that he developed a fear of school because of his distrust of a certain masculine teacher. The fault of this teacher was that he spoke loudly, intimidating the child. If this concern were not tackled, the young man might have established distrust of officials, teachers, and academics in general, and even vehicles where he was driven to school. Early on, he may have developed general anxiety and even agoraphobia that would keep him from leaving the house.

Trauma and stress are related together. Trauma-physical, emotional, or psychological causes stress. Trauma can be described as a sudden, unexpected event (but also expected to be abused), which disturbs the body and mind for a short or long time. As such, body and mind disruptions are known as' pain' or' bad stress.' These stresses can be felt for a short time or can be sustained when chronic. At such times, the body becomes used to stress, and the person with that discomfort feels that it is comfortable. Traumatic stress is a term not known in the language of medical diagnosis.

PTSD known as (Post-traumatic stress disorder) is a medical condition understood. This occurs because of stress after a traumatic event, as the name suggests. Some threats a person has or can be seen can cause symptoms of post-traumatic stress disorder. The syndrome was made up of a cluster of symptoms, including hallucinations, flashes of trauma, improved irritability, and sensitivity to minor noise, sleep disorders, preventing any image or memory, which reminds the trauma patient. If these symptoms do not occur simultaneously, the person will not suffer from the post-traumatic stress disorder. Such symptoms were common in people who have experienced road accidents, natural disasters, such as earthquakes and hurricanes, fires, torture, physical and sexual violence, and war.

Any situation that is viewed as harmful by the unconscious mind from the viewpoint of the human body and mind is considered traumatic and, therefore, stressful. So if a parent, for example, cries at a child that the mind of the child will report as traumatic, depending on the disposition of the child. This experience can be regarded as traumatic, but not as a life-threatening event. Even if the screaming experience were short-lived, it could remain alive for a long time in the child's mind. This can continue to affect the child's thinking and behavior until the problem is dealt with. Bullying, neglect, refusal, physical punishment, and humiliation are examples of events that the intellect perceives as not threats to life, but as a threat to freedom. Although individual events have a strong impact, repeated perceived threats could become stressful to the victim. Each experience that creates fear or rage and is suppressed is accompanied by traumatic events in mind.

A mid-aged lady once came to see me for issues arising from her immediate family's five deaths in a short space of time. Her childhood was uninterrupted and happy, which was reflected in her relationship with her husband and kids. Although she had no life-threatening issues, the losses were distressing for her. The body had to suit the mind, so she became depressed and could not focus on daily life.

If a kid is brought up in an intense strict climate, the child's mind experiences a loss of freedom. It happens unintentionally. If the child's life does not have strong acceptance, strictness becomes a trauma. When an emotional expression is lost, psychological stress is felt.

Neurotransmitters are called hormones and chemicals that control our physiological activities. Bad stress happens when a hormone called cortisol is inappropriately secreted in the body. The role of this hormone is to mobilize the body to prevent or counter any danger to the senses (view, smell, touch, hearing, and taste). Whether the threat is real or imaginary is a different matter. The mind considers the threatening object's image as actual. When someone was bullied a few years ago, the photographs held in the mind of the individual the events alive. If the person experiences another circumstance or individual who unintentionally reminds them of bullying incidents, the person tends to feel the same way he did during the first incident. The net effect of many related unpleasant experiences influences the individual's current perception, thinking, and behavior.

Within our consciousness, the mental-body relation of traumatic stress is not understood to us. An individual may have problems with a physical or psychological character, completely ignoring the duty of the unconscious part of our mind. I have seen in my research, among other problems triggered by traumatic stress, adult cases of weathering, social phobia, high blood pressure, low testosterone levels, diabetes, blood disorders, depression, anxiety, eating disorders, and addictions. To forget an unpleasant experience because it took place a number of years ago is not an excuse for the unconscious mind not to be influenced.

Research shows that relaxation works under all stress situations. Daily relaxation practice is effective because it has the same effect as unpleasant experiences. This affects the body and the mind cumulatively. Like a bank balance, the "relaxation balance" provides a solution for future tension. Speaking of particularly traumatic events with medical research or therapy neutralizes the emotional impact of the encounters. If so many negative experiences are neutralized, the perception, thinking, and behavior of the individual changes.

During natural disasters such as earthquakes, about 40 to 50% of the population tends to develop Post-Traumatic Stress Disorder symptoms. The other people who have experienced the same trauma will not experience symptoms but can continue to bear the emotional distress for an indefinite period. Psychiatrists note that 30% of individuals with anxiety disorders do not have previous life traumatic experiences. It is the population that has no symptoms immediately following a 30 percent trauma. 70 percent of depressed people experience stressful life events.

PTSD affects roughly 0.4% to 1% of the population at any given time. It is a common and undiagnosed disorder of mental health. Henderson, Andrews, and Hall published research in Australia in the Australian and New Zealand Psychiatry Review in 2000. The report concluded that PTSD patients are 26 times higher with mood disorders such as depression than the overall population; 37 times higher with generalized anxiety, 28.6 times higher with panic disorder, and 6.5 times higher with alcohol abuse. PTSD also makes a person more vulnerable to developing symptoms when subsequently exposed to minor traumatic events left untreated. Research also shows that a calm person is less effective than others when trauma occurs.

What you experience as' work stress' or 'family stress' or 'road rage' is situation stress that has its roots elsewhere. If you are comfortable enough, these interactions have little tension. So if you regularly practice some sort of relaxation, you unconsciously absorb the effects of relaxation. This cumulative relaxation serves as an emotional shield at difficult times. You are less prone to traumatic stress or work stress or frustration on the lane. Most PTSD claims go to insurance tribunals. Before recently, these cases had been paid overly large sums of money in Ireland. The unknown fact is that the context and the temperament of the person involved are of paramount importance in how the accident affects them. A person born in a weak, dysfunctional family is in a constant state of stress. The trauma of this kind can lead to PTSD symptoms more intensively than someone who is a healthy, safe, and loving person.

COMMON FEELINGS FROM TRAUMA THAT FUEL PTSD SYMPTOMS

If a traumatic event occurs, it shakes us in the middle and often generates unanswered questions. In a futile attempt to answer these questions, special emotions emerge as a way to explain the incomprehensible incident and to leave a mixed bag of feelings behind.

The simple truth, people want answers, want power, and don't like the unknown. Traumas are events that essentially are beyond our control and make us feel powerless at its very heart. This impotence can be immense so that it is in our very nature to create stories about the traumatic event and the parts that make no sense to us in order to gain a false sense of control. We tend to fill the holes in the traumatic experience that has run counter to our moral code and the way we live in the world. Such generally unreliable, false responses to the discrepancies produce strong questions to address, "why has this horrific incident taken place?" The obviously innocuous question is why it is effective and tenacious in keeping the symptoms of PTSD alive and healthy.

If we wonder why we are faced with a phenomenon for which we can never really have the answers, we build our stories. Such tales catalyze false ideas and desires that overwhelm the natural feelings, making the healing process so much harder from traumatic experiences. Traumas may establish two different, natural, and manufactured emotional categories. Natural feelings are the emotions that most people feel in the same situation, whereas the invented emotions are those we build to help us understand the traumatic event, even if it doesn't exist. Rare natural feelings can be fear and sorrow, while common ones might be blame, shame, and guilt.

Let's look closer. Let's look closer. While in action in Afghanistan, Charlie was ordered to drive the third truck by his Platoon Sergeant, while he was usually in the first vehicle. He challenged this decision to the maximum extent he could, creating a situation in which he understood the path. The determination of his command remained.

While on the move, the first truck hit an IED right before his eyes as in slow motion. The blast rocked the entire vehicle, but the only death was to kill two and injure three of those in the first truck. One of the KIA's drivers was the waiting father, who went into the hospital in three weeks to see his wife and to give birth, as well as Charlie's best friend.

The normal emotions of this traumatic event could be depression, fear, and anger using this example. That's where it begins to get tricky. When asked what natural emotions would be, most people would quickly respond by saying culpability, guilt, sorrow, and rage. In this case, guilt and blame would be emotions generated. Charlie will feel sorrow, pain, disappointment, fear, and anger at the loss of his friend. The remorse and shame easily associated with this would, however, be generated because Charlie did nothing wrong. His friend's death was not his fault; no ill will or malice occurred. The only natural thing is remorse, blame, or shame if the person does something wrong and takes responsibility. For example, if somebody was at your home for a dinner party and stole the heirloom necklace of your grandmother, then guilt, shame, or blame would be normal.

When Charlie is left tangled with his loss ' natural emotions, depending on how he expresses them and how he approaches the traumatic experience, it is important that he does not build beliefs and feelings from people. If he cannot ask himself why or some derivative of this issue, he walks a slippery slope through creating stories and emotions that can trigger or intensify the symptoms of PTSD.

If Charlie is socially adept, quickly gets handled, robust has no full trauma, and had a powerful support system, there is a good chance that he will organically handle the natural feeling while he is going through the chagrin loop.

Unfortunately, it's all too easy to create manufactured emotions. When Charlie is not able to work through natural feelings and ends up questioning "why did this happen?" and continues to repeat the experience in his mind, again and again, there is a strong possibility that artificial emotions will develop.

Manufactured emotions are dangerous because they develop unhealthy beliefs about us, the world, and others. Such maladaptive convictions are called stuck points that hold us in our negative thoughts and feelings around the world, which often intensify PTSD symptoms by an action like kerosene. Stuck points can be consuming all of them.

Stuck points are formed by the feelings generated by the traumatic experience and the myths created to make sense of it. It often goes against our way of being in the world when trauma arises. Many people have been raised to believe that good things happen to good people, bad things don't really happen to the weak, or they don't happen to me. Therefore, if there is trauma, it can test our moral and philosophical values and often cause us to change our views about ourselves, the universe, or both. "If something wrong happened, it must be because I am bad and there's something wrong with me," or "The world is bad and it's impossible to be trusted as I thought it could," in other words, these little nasty beliefs are known as "stuck points" are nourished based on manufactured feelings. All that Charlie told himself was stuck in points. There are ten stuck points from his story that can be mentioned above. The good news was that there is an evidence-based therapy that can help undo the stuck points, extinguish the emotions generated, and change the normal sensations. It is called cognitive processing therapy, a specialized procedure for PTSD that addresses stuck points and generated emotions directly. If you are interested in seeking a clinician trained in this treatment method, he can really help.

Although this was just one example of how generated emotions are catalyzed, the same principle does apply to any traumatic event. There are many trauma feelings, and it is important to identify the real from the manufactured. This can change the course and symptoms of PTSD.

CHAPTER SEVEN

PTSD TREATMENT, SAFE ALTERNATIVES

Big money is made from dealing with PTSD. In the news, Post-Traumatic Stress Disorder has become a marketing tool for all manner of medical medications, whether through services sponsored by the Federal Government or private insurers. More importantly, this form of PTSD diagnosis is based on clinical therapy, not medical science, or true human knowledge of what our military personnel and women and certain civilians suffered from.

There are a few organizations, for the most humanistic approach to PTSD therapy, that focus on helping people get through the traumatic experiences and helping people build a stable, successful life for themselves.

For example, "Veterans find peace with equine therapy" was the subject of a recent channel ten news section in Sarasota, Florida, on the Circle V Ranch and rehabilitation center in Dade City. The mission of this ranch is to support veterans and first responders with alternative treatment (Alternative to the use of pharmaceutical products). The farm deals with equine therapy in order to support the veteran and the horse, and through this service, the veteran will advance throughout his life. Another counselor at the center states from the news that "they start to reconnect with each other as they interact with the horse. They will begin to communicate with the community when they connect with themselves; thus, they can start reconnecting with their families." However, the ranch offers support to the family, given that PTSD symptoms impact all.

Therapy for mental health has become the leading approach to PTSD. The FDA warns of delusions, hallucinations, mania, paranoia, suicidal thoughts, homicidal ideas, violence, and many more, which come with psychiatric medications, and for some, it involuntarily activates when a person is exposed to the adverse effects of the drugs. Staying in a psychiatric ward is an additional stigma, an additional financial burden, and another chance to diagnose and treat the patient with medications.

Dr. Gary G. Kohl has recently published a paper that is most applicable to those who have been branded Psychotic PTSD, Bipolar, Depressed, Manic, and who otherwise have been opened up for diagnosis, position on medication, and psychiatric treatment. A specialist in traumatic stress conditions, brain function, and non-pharmaceutical approaches to mental health, neuro sender disorders, food additive neurotoxicity, and psychotropic drug issues.

This benefits patients who have had adverse drug reactions have developed dependence, have symptoms of withdrawal, and/or who experience toxicity from the medications themselves. In Dr. Kohl's post, titled "Psychiatric Hospitals: On being well in 'insane areas,' if there are safety and insanity, how can we know it?"This is a popular study published in 1973 by D. L. Roshenan, which exposed the serious weaknesses of eight psychiatric hospitals at that time as professional people, like Roshenan itself, fake the symptom of hearing and admitted themselves to 12 separate psychiatric hospitals. 23 of the 41 patients were suspected by a doctor to be fraudulent, and 10 were accused of being both by a psychologist and another staff member. "From this, 41 patients were thus rescued from being diagnosed with mental illness and shielded from the altering mental effects of psychiatric drugs. Therefore, concepts of health or folly sometimes may be incorrect." Health and folly have cultural variations, for one society, what is seen as common can be seen as very aberrant in another. As just one example, there was a renowned experiment with American and British psychiatrists and diagnostic discrepancies in each region. All researchers conducted the same interviews with a psychiatric group of patients. Psychiatry was much more often treated by American physicians than by British psychiatry in this series of cases.

"Psychiatric diagnoses even erroneously convey personal, legal, and social stigmas which are impossible to shake and which often last for a lifetime." For everyone with PTSD symptoms or any other symptoms of mental health, alternative treatments are available, and medical professionals work to help you overcome this difficulty. It promises more than it was years ago. The information is available here to help you and your family gets all the facts before they decide your care. There are advocates who can help you to access this information more easily, as they, too, are committed to ensuring the right to full information.

WHAT ARE THE CAUSES OF PTSD?

In order to understand the whole theory of post-traumatic stress disorder, the root causes of PTSD must be discussed first, as is commonly referred to. This is a collection of symptoms that were first described in the 1860-1865, American Civil War. Physicians began noticing signs on both sides of the conflict that stopped veterans from re-entering civilian life. Some of the symptoms were serious hallucinations, usually related to noises and battle memories. Many veterans have suffered panic attacks that we now consider to be some things would trigger battle memories, like a gunshot or a snapshot like a twig-and it would trigger PTSD. The symptoms of PTSD have been more widely recognized over the years since the Civil War. During World War I, for example, it was noticed that veterans returning from War during Europe seemed to be transformed in such a way that the people on the front door could not understand. This state was called shell shock. By the time of World War II, the army knew more than well the origins of PTSD and began working on treatment methods.

Nevertheless, post-traumatic stress disorder is not limited to soldiers alone. Anyone who has had an incident of a deep emotional wound in their life will develop PTSD symptoms. For example, a woman who has been raped might experience symptoms; if she is around strange men, or if she walks in a dark corridor, she might have panic attacks, which are identical to where her attack took place. People who have experienced a major natural disaster may also have symptoms of PTSD. Earthquake victims, for instance, can be intense fear if anything shakes the world, whether it is just as innocent as a street steamroller or a real earthquake. PTSD can also be caused by car accidents or by a violent attack on someone else. Doctors confirmed that small children who underwent surgery had experienced PTSD symptoms subsequently. Similarly, people with gunshot wounds may experience PTSD symptoms.

It is also important to note that not everybody with a significant traumatic event experiences PTSD symptoms. It is encouraging to know that there are new treatments available for those who have developed symptoms of PTSD that, in most cases, show remarkable results and enable the sufferer to return to the appearance of normal life. There is hope for those who suffer from the sometimes worsening condition-life can again be nice, and you can feel normal.

Rachael was 14 when she went to a residential bulimia treatment clinic with anorexic symptoms and drug addiction. She recalled a traumatic memory that had been buried for years during her initial treatment process. While Rachael was on a family holiday with her father at the age of 11, a gang of unknown men attacked her. Since she had repressed this memory, she had told nobody about the event and hadn't received social assistance or an outlet to express and heal her trauma pain.

After four years at the residential center, Rachael came to us with the shame on the body, bulimic symptoms and self-blaming. For the sexual trauma, she blamed herself, felt guilty because she was at the time without adult supervision, and believed that she encouraged the attackers to be too friendly. The self-responsibility was not surprising given her early mistaken interpretations or decisions of herself. From an early age, Rachael claimed that everything was somehow "her fault." At the age of eighteen, she was completely separated from her body and refused to accept her femininity. Her interpersonal relationships and accomplishments of intimacy were severe problems, particularly in romantic relationships, and she could not feel worthy or enjoy these experiences. We first helped Rachael reframe her negative self-image and change skewed assumptions about the traumatic event, enabling her to overcome disgraceful thinking about her corpse and discontinue self-blaming. Her bonding activity was a way to "fill herself emotionally" metaphorically and then force out and hide certain of her feelings of disgust and self-loathing. Therapy provided positive self-affirmations to counteract her negative feelings about herself and her body to counter this behavior.

We have participated in a number of experiential and body-oriented approaches for coping with trauma and eating disorders. Psychodrama's coping strategy was used to give her a sense of power over her husband and the violent situation. Through Yoga and movement exercises, she began to connect better with her body and discovered that moving and enjoying her body is all right. After a couple of years, Rachael was used to proving that she was able to accept it and to be treated lovingly in a non-abusive manner, and that handling it was not to be feared.

Rachael was able to remove her bulimic symptoms at the conclusion of our research together and expressed a stronger sense of love and acceptance for her body. Rachael has been able to better understand and ease many of her eating disorders by dealing with problems around her traumatic sexual encounter and learn how to manage her feelings in a healthier way. This case study is just one example of how sexual assault or trauma caused an eating disorder.

There is an increasing rate of sexual abuse in women, with lifetime sexual abuse estimates ranging from 15 to 25 percent in the general female population (Lesserman 2005). Sexual abuse and trauma may occur throughout a lifetime and is generally characterized, given variable definitions, as inappropriate sexual contact, from exposure or fondling to rape (Bagley, 1990). Some circumstances of sexual trauma have been linked to increased eating disorders, particularly if the parents have been involved in the sexual trauma or if it has happened many times, (Murray and Waller, 2002). Sexual abuse may not have immediate consequences because emotional trauma can persist when the abuse stops. In the social connections, the influence of such violence can be seen very clearly, as abused persons are likely to express distress and concerns surrounding love and sexual intimacy with others. Other violence or trauma effects may remain more hidden and concealed, but may also be toxic and harmful.

It involves the creation of the body's intense disgust and hatred, as well as an overwhelming sense of unpredictable events in one's life. In essence, previous experiences of sexual abuse or trauma will affect how you function in your body and eventually survive and engage in the world. A history of sexual abuse or trauma has been shown to be a risk factor for a wide range of physical disorders or psychopathologies, including depression and obsessive-compulsive symptoms and low self-esteem. Importantly, both researchers and clinicians generally agree that trauma arising from a history of sexual abuse may play a role in disrupting body image and eating disturbing effects of sexual intercourse related to eating disorders Prevalence of sexual abuse estimates in individuals with eating disorders is variable. That number is possibly disturbingly underestimated because of its personal nature, the secrecy, shame, and humiliation associated with sexual harassment. Research has found that patients with an eating disorder and a prior history of sexual abuse and trauma are more likely to report self-destructive behavior and impulsiveness. Furthermore, some individuals may not actively access the experience of sexual abuse, that is, it may not be expressible or accessible to memory, because of the manipulative nature of sexual assault in most situations, and sex trauma survivors may feel powerless and have little control over their own bodies. As many people with eating disorders can see a need for self-control, a need to gain control over the body can occur when paired with a history of sexual abuse. Through the intake of food, the abused person can feel that their body is under his or her own control for at least a limited period.

For women with eating disorders and a history of sexual harassment or violence, frustration, and lack of acceptance of their own identity and femininity is prevalent. Some may believe that their bodies are too attractive/provocative and seductive to their abusers and therefore blame their bodies for the traumatic experience, which has negative consequences for female sexuality. The appetite of the body may be a way to express or punish the body's frustration at the experience itself. The low level of sexual desire and lack of anorexia treatment that act as a way to return to a childlike state where sexuality and femininity problems cannot be addressed that trigger emotional and psychological distress. In fact, eating disorders and body degradation can be a way to deny desire and avoid painful feelings and memories from abusing and traumatic violations.

Individuals with bulimia have reported the greatest association between food disorders and sexual abuse. Bulimia has been associated with increased prevalence with more serious histories of sexual abuse in tandem with other clinical co-morbidity and, in particular, substance abuse.

Why bulimia?

Purging may serve as a way of purifying and as a metaphor for the removal of unpleasant or "dirty" feelings and experiences from the body. For instance, a person might feel which vomiting is the only way to get rid of the feelings and memories of the unwanted sexual encounter they experienced and experience relief.

What are some of the key elements to treat this particular population? As any therapeutic relationship, it is of utmost importance to promote empathy and to establish a trustful, healthy, and caring therapist-client dyad. Past traumatic experiences may have left the consumer with a lack of trust in others and a disturbing view of the world. To patients who have attachment issues, the boundaries of the therapeutic relationship must be clearly defined so that the client is not threatened or frustrated and that he feels he is in a safe place to express and heal his feelings and pain.

Throughout therapy, it is important to recognize how disordered behaviors are designed or intended and finally help the person to realize that these behaviors until they can function in a productive and emotionally healthy way are a needed survival mechanism. Finally, the consumer understands that the eating disorder is a true gift in all aspects of life for development and learning. The psychiatrist will look at why a client is bingeing, which is likely due to an effort to deal with the feelings of violence or to cleanse the body of feelings of dissatisfaction. Furthermore, since control issues are a central issue in this population, emphasis on perceived control in therapy should be addressed by encouraging clients to take an active approach to their therapy and allowing them to decide to stop if the conversation is too unpleasant. Ultimately, because motivation is an antithesis to discouragement, the therapist can help the client to understand that they are not to blame, that they cannot change the past, and instead can actively pursue the goal of healing from trauma, regain a sense of personal strength and femininity and learn to nurture and enjoy their bodies again.

Additional specific methods are recommended for exploring with abused-eat disordered customers, including exercises that increase awareness, control, and ownership of one's own body. For some survivors of sexual abuse or trauma, verbal therapy may be less successful, particularly when trauma happens early in development, as it is possible that memories are not verbally encoded. Psychodrama, movement, yoga, and other body-oriented treatments can be more productive for these clients since they can enable the patient to communicate and enjoy his body again and to revive his sexuality. Relaxation therapy can also be used to build an understanding of the many linked, caring, and deserving facets of one's own body. In the course of therapy, guided imaging can also be used to help customer familiarization with a safe place that provides them with a feeling of safety and comfort, especially with fear and anger release techniques, such as the use of tackle drums in the healing of safe place, could also increase a sense of empowerment rather than feeling that you are a victim. The approach used together with the stated therapeutic goals will rely on the individual's specific experiences, the stage of their rehabilitation, their tolerance to change, and their present sense of health.

CHAPTER EIGHT

THE BENEFITS OF HYPNOTHERAPY AS PTSD THERAPY

The quality of a person's life can be severely affected by post-traumatic stress disorder (PTSD). Numerous PTSD treatments with hypnosis are one of the choices. Is hypnotherapy an appropriate way to overcome PTSD, and what does it bring about?

What is Post-Treatment Stress Disorder?

Traumatic people may feel a sense of loss, anxiety, panic, and fear. Whenever these symptoms last a very long time and tend to affect the quality of life, they are referred to as post-traumatic stress disorder.

PTSD is characterized by the re-experience of traumatic incidents and hallucinations, the inability to deal with stress, and heightened fear or anxiety. Reminders such as fast breathing, intense physical reactions, and general apathy are also typical for PTSD.

Events like War, death of a loved one, natural disasters, children's problems and abuse, kidnapping, sexual abuse, domestic violence, and aviation crashes often lead to this condition. Any other life-changing and the devastating incident may also contribute to PTSD.

How can PTSD sufferers Hypnosis Aid People with PTSD be recommended to try hypnotherapy because it helps in several ways?

Many of the effects experienced by PTSD are close to what happens during the hypnotherapy. Individuals with PTSD respond to hypnosis quite well and have access to the guidance of the therapist to painful memories. These memories can be restructured by hypnosis to prevent future PTSD symptoms.

Hypnosis and self-hypnosis are also great instruments for managing PTSD recurrences.

Various studies have been conducted to test these arguments. Hypnosis treatment is at least as effective as alternative treatments for PTSD, such as psychotherapy, scientific evidence on the efficacy of hypnotherapy. A study was conducted in 2005 in order to compare hypnotherapy against other therapies widely used to relieve symptoms of PTSD. The findings vary from person to person based on how suggestible the individual with PTSD is. Sixty-seven PTSD participants agreed to take part in the research. Hypnotherapy, cognitive behavioral therapy, and counseling were the approaches used for these cases.

Research showed that people diagnosed with hypnotherapy as well as cognitive behavioral therapy, had fewer signs of PTSD six months after the session. Persons receiving advice alone had a higher level of lifestyle problems related to PTSD.

Those with hypnotherapy have reported lower re-experience incidences of the traumatic event.

People with PTSD will display up to 93% recovery after six hypnotherapy sessions.

The number is 72 percent with cognitive behavioral therapy after 22 sessions and 38 percent with psychotherapy after 600 sessions.

These research and figures show that hypnosis can be used to improve the quality of life of those with past trauma and unable to heal.

Individuals with PTSD are potentially more easily hypnotized than others. It raises the value of this treatment option for people suffering from post-traumatic stress disorders.

10 TIPS FOR UNDERSTANDING SOMEONE WITH PTSD

PTSD makes it difficult to communicate. Most survivors cannot find words to describe what they feel. Even when they do, it's very natural for them not to share their experience comfortably. Elements of embarrassment, terror, anger, remorse, and sorrow sometimes impede a calm, concentrated debate.

Friends and families (and anyone else who is not the PTSD trigger but stands by while someone is trying to cure) need a PTSD language translation. Through awareness, understanding, and empathy, you will have the best time to respond and connect during the healing process to your beloved PTSD. The more helpful and supportive you can be from the PTSD point of view. Now is the time for understanding, tolerance, and empathy.

#1–Power is information. Knowing the triggering mechanism, mental trauma reactions, PTSD warning signs, and symptoms, and the treatment options available to PTSD help you to understand better, maintain and direct your loved PTSD through diagnosis, care, and healing.

We need you to be straightforward, focused and updated.

#2-Trauma affects us, trauma changes us. Upon trauma, we want to believe–as you do–that life will return like it was; that we can go on like what we were. It doesn't work like that. Trauma leaves a profound and indelible soul mark. Trauma cannot be felt, and a psychological transition cannot be witnessed.

Expect that we will be modified. Consider our evolutionary need. Join us on this trip. Help us.

#3-Our personality has been concealed by the PTSD. One of PTSD's biggest problems is that it takes over our whole view. We don't see clearly anymore. We don't see the world as we saw it before the trauma. It's dangerous, volatile, and challenging at every moment.

Remind us carefully and give us the opportunity to engage in an identity outside PTSD and trauma.

#4-We are not in our true self anymore. In the face of trauma, our true self-isolation and a healing self tend to shield us.

Believe in us, even if they are momentarily buried, our true selves still remain.

#5—How we act can't help us. We do not always monitor because we run on a kind of autopilot. PTSD is a survival mode exacerbated. We have feelings that make us nervous and overwhelmed. We behave in defense of those emotions that we are unable to control.

We often cannot avoid the frustration, tears, or other destructive habits that are so difficult for you to bear. Be patient with us.

#6-We can't make sense. Because our perspective is dominated by fear, we do not always think straight or follow the advice of those who do.

Even if your words don't seem to touch us, keep reaching out. You never know when we'll think of what you do, and it's going to ease, lead, relax or encourage us.

#7-We can't 'get it' just. It's easy to imagine a time from outside and memories fade away and pain is relegated to the past of a life. Unfortunately, nothing fades with PTSD. Our bodies are not going to let us forget. Due to the rising chemicals that enhance every memory, we can no longer walk away from the past than you can.

Honor our struggle with events to make peace. Do not hurry us. Do not pressure us. Trying to speed up our rehabilitation will only make us add more to it.

#8-We're not living in denial! Living with PTSD takes a tremendous effort. We know something is wrong even if we don't admit it. When you approach us and deny that there is an issue that really codes for: "I do my best." To do what you say will need too much time, separate the emphasis from what holds us together. Sometimes just waking up and continuing our day-to-day routine is the first step in recovery.

Reduce our tension by providing us with a safe place where we can find support.

#9—We hate you not. We hate you not. Contrary to the ways we can behave when you intervene, we know that you are not the source of the problem somewhere inside. Sadly, we may use your face as the PTSD picture at the moment. Because we can't deal with our PTSD problems directly, it's sometimes easier to address you.

Keep contacting us. We need you! We need you!

#10—Your presence is important. PTSD creates a great loneliness. It makes a difference in our post-traumatic state to know that there are people who will stand by us. It's vital that while we're gunning, not responding, you are still there, no matter what.

OVERCOMING FEAR AFTER HAVING TRAUMATIC EXPERIENCES

Traumatic experiences cause changes in your psychological system and cause disturbances in your behavior. You have no confidence to go forward with many traumatic life experiences, and you are always scared of everything, and even after more than many assurances that you are always secure, you cannot feel safe.

Even if you do not suffer from post-traumatic stress disorder, you appear in many cases to be overcome by anxiety after experiencing traumatic experiences that have negatively affected your life. Since losing your faith, you can't trust your own decision.

It is very difficult to overcome anxiety following traumatic experiences. Such traumatic experiences can affect your lives and behavior, depending on the type of experiences you have had and your personality and life history.

Today, due to the insights of psychiatrists and psychologist Carl Jung and his system of dream interpretation, you can overcome any fears.

The unconscious mind, which has a divine source and shows God's existence, in reality, creates your dreams. Science is now able to explain theological myths, and religion will teach us the true meaning of scientific truths.

The unconscious mind lets you read the minds of the people, predict the future, and alter your destiny depending on your attitude. You must learn with wisdom to conquer all fear.

You will meet people you can trust and help everyone around you pursue the same psychotherapy and mental transformation cycle you practice through dream therapy, which also acts as spiritual purification as it allows you to be happier.

You will feel safe for those like you who practice dream therapy because you know that they obey the divine guidance and understand the importance of truth and goodness.

When someone starts practicing dream therapy, this person understands that aggression and selfishness have nothing good. Everyone undergoes a deep transformation process and learns how to eradicate their crazy patterns and achieve a higher level of knowledge.

This understanding lasts a lifetime. None forgets this lesson after gaining knowledge of what is bad and after understanding the importance of goodness. You would be surrounded by people who understand these realities because their friends like you want to pursue dream therapy.

This is a very common occurrence. Whenever someone knows the true value of dreams and how meaningful they are, someone else in their vicinity pays attention to their success and also to dream therapy. You're going to be with people who follow your example.

On the other hand, you will never believe in illusions after you understand the functioning of the human brain and human behavior. You'll remember that all people inherited our primitive consciousness as an absurd and evil anti-consciousness.

The anti-consciousness did not evolve as our human consciousness did. Whenever it invades our minds, we listen to its senseless feelings. By consciousness, you will eliminate your anti-consciousness, but you know that other people are always influenced or controlled by their anti-consciousness.

Until you know what is in the human brain, you will never look at human beings the way you did. You're going to know what human behavior defines. You will only understand many things by watching the reactions of other men. You won't fall into pits that ignorant people can't see after having this dream.

Therefore, based on the knowledge you have, you can conquer your fears. So you'll know what is dangerous and why it's dangerous to you.

You will realize that you have to be afraid of many people and of many life situations. The more you know about human nature and the negative influence of the anti-consciousness, the more afraid you will be.

This fear, however, will not cause paralysis but works as protection. You must be frightened when you face dangerous situations. Your fear protects you from error by neglect and distraction.

Once your personality has been changed and the traumas of the past removed, your fears are not based on ignorance, but on knowledge. They will warn you protectively that you are in danger. At the same time, you will know that you are free because in all circumstances you will know how to behave and always avoid what is negative.

The consciousness cycle in the visions of the unconscious spiritual mind opens your mind to a new dimension. You can see all that is concealed behind the cynicism and ignorance mask. You can also understand that awareness is stronger.

You know that moral success is redemption because it helps you overcome all positive problems. You reach a new level of consciousness, far from the wretched constraints of animal life.

You stop thinking like ignorant people. You understand art, faith, and philosophy's true beauty. You know that only perfect things are complete. You don't fear any threat. You just know you're going to win.

The satisfaction with your behavior and the stronger personality that you have after dream treatment will give you an enormous advantage that most people don't have. Many people make many mistakes and regret that they have done what they did many times.

You're never going to make mistakes. You're just going to act with wisdom.

This value will always help you to feel safe and secure. You will not be afraid to show the world your true face. You're never going to have to wear a mask. You are going to be happy because you are higher than the ignorant world and so different.

You're never going to be ashamed of yourself. You're always going to be proud of your acts.

You're not going to be arrogant, of course. You will be sad about the world and determined to save all.

You'll find the right person for you, too. It's a surprise. Most people never find their perfect match because their personality never changes. To find your perfect match, you must avoid being dominated by your anti-consciousness. You will be able to discover the right person because you will through the wild side.

Dream therapy helps you find the right match or improve your existing relationship. Your spouse will follow the same consciousness cycle, and your relationship will be fine.

The unconscious mind is always helping all dreamers to come together perfectly even if they are following dream therapy because they are mentally ill, because they want their anger to be removed or because they don't want to have a relationship for any other reason. This is because love is the most important thing in our lives.

On the other hand, love and insanity are intimately linked. The unconscious mind still wants to help us find the right person to maintain health.

Which means you'll have the support of a trustworthy person. You are always a loyal partner, and you love life for your perfect match.

The unconscious mind allows you to achieve your goal. Completion means complete satisfaction in life, satisfaction with yourself, and your future.

Since you are with the ideal person and content with yourself, you are in a privileged position. This idea will give you a good mood all the time. You must start a new life, completely different from the previous life.

Some of the common symptoms of PTSD include repetitive incidents, emotional triggers, and anxiety, the flickering of the traumatic event, high-level physical reaction to the incident such as rapid respiration, beating heart, muscle tension, nausea, sweating, etc. Patients with PTSD tend to avoid attending the accident site in order to avoid confrontation with trauma again. These people also feel disconnected from society and emotionally consumed. Victims of PTSD also feel that the return of normal life activities will be minimal. Patients with PTSD find it difficult to sleep or stay asleep. They would also find it difficult to focus on things, experience unexpected bouts of frustration, and be easily shocked. The individual may even experience suicidal tendencies in more extreme cases of PTSD.

Treatment options

There are many treatment options available in the case of PTSD. Both therapies are based on rigorous clinical strategies, which include the patient opening up and sharing trauma-related emotions. Patients are also taught how to treat PTSD symptoms effectively. Our dedicated team of psychologists allows PTSD patients to understand behavioral patterns associated with this disorder. We also include close friends and family members so that the individual can provide consistent emotional support. They also incorporate these holistic therapies with appropriate medication to help PTSD patients more efficiently. Effective medications such as Zoloft and Prozac are usually prescribed for symptoms of PTSD. The therapies incorporate medications and therapy for the root cause of the disease. It is important to find the right therapist to treat PTSD successfully. We have experience in our clinic and a team of dedicated psychiatrists who are able to deal with cases that are even very sensitive.

THE ATTACHMENT THEORY

Discover the Basics of Your Actual Relationships by Your Attachment Style using the Emotional Focused Therapy (EFT)

Greg Watson

reparation, damages, or monetary loss due to the information herein, either directly or indirectly.

Respective authors own all copyrights not held by the publisher.

The information herein is offered for informational purposes solely, and is universal as so. The presentation of the information is without contract or any type of guarantee assurance.

The trademarks that are used are without any consent, and the publication of the trademark is without permission or backing by the trademark owner. All trademarks and brands within this book are for clarifying purposes only and are the owned by the owners themselves, not affiliated with this document

Attachment theory can be analyzed and dissected in many ways, but it is presented in its simplest form to highlight the complexities of interpersonal relationships between people. It can start with ties between parents and children, friendships and, of course, romantic relations. Generally, there are four sides to the attachment theory that most models use to define: free, busy, disintegrating, and frightening.

There is a lot of literature these days about how parents challenge children. Unfortunately, much of that literature generally does not discuss children with specific parental needs and unique understanding of parenting. A child diagnosed with behavioral communication disorders, oppositional defiant disorders, or even depression needs to understand the underlying factors that cause the behavior, not the behavior itself.

Attachment Parenting is a concept based on the theory of attachment in developmental psychology. According to the theory of attachment, strong emotional bonds with children contribute to stable and empathic adult connections.

CHAPTER ONE

WHAT IS ATTACHMENT THEORY?

Attachment theories

Theories of Attachment as a parent and new-born parents, we have spent reading and reading a lot of time exploring different childhood ideas, trying to find out what's best for children and what works for the families. All reading in the world cannot prepare us for the almost overwhelming emotional intensity which comes with hearing this first scream, holding a child for the first time, or any one of the many first "firsts" of parenthood. While you have had many relationships before you meet your child, your first and most significant relationship is with your child, so your connection must be one of a stable bond.

Understanding attachment?

In other words, attachment is an emotional relationship between people. John Bowlby, a psychologist who was the leading attachment theorist, described attachment as' a lasting psychological relation between human beings.' Bowlby theorized that child bonds with parents tend to have an enormous impact on existence. The bond holds the baby attached to the mother and thus increases the child's survival opportunities.

The central tenant for attachment theory is that mothers who relate to their child and are available for the needs of their child develop a sense of security in their child. As the child learns that his/her caregiver is trustworthy, the baby has a safe "home base" to explore his/her world.

The attachment features

When the caregiver leaves a securely attached infant, the child feels safe and is certain to return. If children who are firmly afflicted are frightened, they turn to their caregivers for protection.

Conversely, when parents leave, an ambivalently attached child is distressed because the child cannot rely on the mother or caregiver to be present when it is needed.

Children with avoidant attachment tend to avoid careers or guardians, as the name suggests. If a caregiver punishes a child, he will learn in the future not to seek the help of the caregiver.

Parents and Attachment: One does not have to be a counselor to assess the emotionally stability of a child. The attached child will become stronger and self-esteem more than the less attached child. These attachment types do not suit all of them. Even the most "attached" child often worries about leaving his caregiver, and the ambivalent and avoidant attachment is not very normal. So, what can parents do to encourage children attached?

Attachment Parenting: Pediatrician William Sears is a proponent of attachment for parents and children. He tells us that parental attachment is an approach, not a set of rules, and provides several easy, child-friendly strategies for parental attachment. Dr. Sears recommends "Seven Bs," which help parents start with attachment parenting, they include: "birth bonding, breastfeeding, baby wearing [on sling or baby carrier], baby bedding, belief in the linguistic value of the cries of the baby, care for baby trainers and balance[between baby and your needs]." The aim here is to be sensitive to the needs of your baby and to respond more responsively to his needs so that your relationship can be closer and stronger.

It takes time to connect your child to it, after all you just met it - but when you participate in strategies that encourage physical and emotional proximity to your infant, you'll learn to predict his needs and respond quickly, ensuring that your child knows he can depend on you for comfort and safety.

ATTACHMENT THEORY BASICS

The term "attachment" is commonly used in parenting publications and often appears in parenting discussions. All of us have an understanding of what parent-child attachment is about, but "attachment" has a very specific meaning to child development theory and science. In reality, a whole line of research focused solely on the theory of attachment. So I'd give some insight on what psychologists mean when they talk about attachment.

Two psychologists— John Bowlby and Mary Ainsworth developed the academic understanding of attachments. After seeing the trauma and psychological damage caused by children separated from their parents due to war and disease in post-World War II, Bowlby became interested in parent-child attitudes. At the time, parents were often not allowed, sometimes for months, to see their hospitalized children.

He started to theorize that infants and children are designed to find closeness to a fastener (usually a parent) due to protection, safety, and care. Infants and young children have to be loyal to their bond, using' attachment behaviors' such as crying, grasping and following. He also theorized that children who encounter parent responses that are dismissive or unresponsive would have psychological problems much more often later on.

Mary Ainsworth, a Bowlby alum, further developed the theory of attachment. She argued that the kind of attachment created depends on the Parent-child interaction. When the parent reacts to the child's safety and security needs, the child learns that the parent can be trusted. By comparison, when the parent's needs are met, the child learns that the parent cannot trust him, and the child can establish ways to cope, such as being over-clingy or avoiding the parent.

The idea that kids will develop an "internal working model" of how relationships are based on attachment to the parent is also an interesting aspect of attachment theory. In other words, if you believe that you can trust your parents to meet your needs, you (not consciously) feel another adult (i.e., teachers, friends) could be trusted too. In the same way, children often create their internal working models. Once their parent is attentive to them, they know they are deserving of caring for themselves.

You may think that all this theory sounds fantastic at this stage, but is there any evidence to support it, and what does all this mean in real life?

Mary Ainsworth began studying and testing her attachment theory in Uganda in the mid-1950s. She followed mothers and babies at home in Uganda for up to nine months, several hours a day. Upon her return to the U.S., she conducted a similar study with a group of American mothers and babies in Baltimore. Finally, she invented a study method called the Strange Situation, which helped researchers to recognize a child's connection to his or her parent.

The Strange Situation generally includes a series of short separations and meetings between the children (typically about 12 months of age) and his / her parent or caregiver (usually the mother). How the child responds to the parent when she returns is important for recognizing the type of attachment. Ainsworth has finally developed three categories of attachments based on the strange situation:

Safe: most children (60%) play happily with their mother in the same room. They normally spend some time near their mother and exploring their world. You use your mother as a "safe base" for discovering your new environment. Once they leave, the children are usually very sad, but when they return, they are quickly calm and comforted by their mother.

Ambivalent: Many children don't use their mother for such a degree as a safe base and try to remain close to her even before separation. Such children become extremely upset when separated. When they meet their mother, they appear to react in ambivalence- they may cry to be taken, but then they seem to push the mother away or not easily soothed.

Avoidant: Some children show their mother a pattern of avoidance. They don't play with their mother while she is in the house, and they show no sadness when she leaves. Such children do not try to find her readily when they encounter their mother.

 Many years later, the concept was established. Such children are often very upset by their mother's separation but exhibit unorganized behavior, as they approach, but then return. They can exhibit actions such as frozen or rolling faces. Children whose mothers have a mental illness or serious trauma have such trends.

It is important to note that most children have their caregivers securely attached. Evidence has shown that children who show signs of unhealthy attachment (i.e., evasive, ambivalent, etc.) mostly have parents who are either unresponsive or inconsistent in their child responses (i.e., responsive, but not always) so that they cannot respond.

I would also like to point out that the philosophy of attachment is distinct from attachment parenting. The psychologists Ainsworth and Bowlby did not develop unique parenting strategies by themselves in the development of attachment theory. The key influencers of the relationship are sensitivity-insensitivity, accessibility-ignorance, acceptance-rejection, and cooperation-interference, Ainsworth wrote.

Attachment parenting is a variation of parenting strategies and values that have been introduced in recent years (not by Ainsworth). Advocates of parental attachment also promote these natural birth, co-sleeping, and babywear. While the original attachment theorists (Ainsworth and Bowlby) concentrated on sensitive, responsive parents, many of the terms used in attachment parenting circles were never listed. In other words, a parent may form a healthy relationship with a child in other ways that only rely on the strategies of "link parenting."

THEORIES OF PARENT/CHILD ATTACHMENT

In the first year of life, an infant has relationships with her parents and caregivers. This first critical year will shape her personality and growth. Based upon her atmosphere and relationships with the people around her, she will build a type of connection that forms her experiences with the rest of her life.

There are four types of fasteners: protected attachment, anxiety-resistant insecure fastening, anxious-avoiding unsafe fastening, and unorganized attachment.

Happy, healthy children usually display a protective attachment. Such children know from previous encounters with caregivers that they can count on the adults to be responsible and consistent with their lives. For instance, when the parent leaves the room, a child learns that the parent is returning by crying. The older child understands that when the parents leave him with a sitter, they come back, and the sitter goes home.

Secure attachment occurs with continuity and contact. To help your child be happy, snuggle, and get close to him as often as possible throughout his childhood. Try to maintain your attitude as calm as possible. Have a regular schedule that gives the child a sense of what's next. For starters, I've got a nap after lunch. Mommy plays with me when I wake up from my nap, and then Dad comes home from work.

Children with a stable style of attachment can make friends and maintain relationships.

Insecure attachment

This category includes children with anxiously resisting, anxiously reactive, and disorganized insecure attachment. These children often appear afraid when in the presence of strangers. Once their parents leave, they scream and cry and feel discomfort. Nevertheless, the child may appear ambivalent when the parent returns.

Such kids have a kind of push-and-pull attitude. We don't know what is going to happen next, so they go back and forth between needing a parent's attention and denying the same attention.

Kids with disorganized attachment are exposed to child abuse or other traumatic events. The parent or caregiver can be as anxious or optimistic, when a child sees the parent worry or the parent is scared, does the child know what to do? Does he/she behave as if the parent needs affection, or is he/she afraid of a dangerous thing?

Stop this situation by offering the love your child needs. If you have personal problems, handle them in therapy but don't take them out with your children. Even if a family tragedy happens, the child must know that he/she can turn to you regardless of what.

Parents can make sure their child is safe by giving him all the love and attention he/she wants as an infant. If you look at the long-term effects of your child's mental health and relationship skills, the benefits of spending quality time and maintaining a consistent lifestyle are worth taking.

THE IMPORTANCE OF SECURE ATTACHMENTS

Attachment may be defined as a relationship or a loving relationship between a child and his or her primal caregiver. All theories of childhood development, stress the bond between the child and parents and other caregivers. One explanation for this importance is the belief that the relationship between child and caregiver is critical for the child's emotional stability and provides a basis for its subsequent impact on the child.

Mary Ainsworth is a prominent figure in the study of attachment behavior. Ainsworth was able to use a technique known as the strange situation to distinguish three separate attachment patterns in children at age eight months. She thought that all children could be listed as one of these three fittings;

(a) Secure fitting

(b) Insecure-resistant fit

(c) Insecure-avoidant fitting;

It is understood that securely attached infants are more socially competent than unstable infants. Research has shown that teachers have improved recognition and social skills in children identified as firmly attached. They also appear less likely to bully other children. How could this be?

The findings that secure attachment is associated with higher self-esteem, autonomy, and empathy towards others can explain enhanced social capacity. Research shows that securely attached children have a good sense of themselves, often identifying positive characteristics while also acknowledging their imperfections. On the other hand, infants with insecurity tend to view themselves negatively or positively (depending on the type of insecure attachment). The quality of secure attachment is likely to make children more enjoyable, popular, and attractive, which leads to better networks of friendship.

Significantly, socially competent and confident people can have better relations with others, while at the same time mingling with peers of similar social standing. It suggests that healthy connection at the start of childhood seems to lead to higher quality and a greater amount of social interaction, which contributes through childhood and youth to continuous social development. It is an ongoing series of events that tend to start in the early development of attachments.

The question is: how do this social potential and enhanced self-esteem develop? In the Piagetian way of thinking, child gains knowledge through environmental action, the more an experience a child can gain, the more he/she learns. Research findings indicate that stable attachment linked to increased childhood exploratory behavior. For example, when kindergarten-age children have put in cognitively challenging situations, those classed as healthy and advanced shows make the problem-solving activities at the age of two more fun and enthusiastic. In contrast, unsafe infants show no such behavior. Safe attachments are more likely to lead to environmental curiosity and increased readiness to explore. John Bowlby describes this phenomenon as the result of a' safe base' from which a child can leave and move away because he/she knows he/she will be back there. Children who have a stable base (i.e., confidence in and a sense of security in their parents ' availability) appear to have a secure attachment and are less likely to be clingy and nervous in a social environment.

It is understood that securely attached people have more cooperation with their parents. This type of behavior may have beneficial effects on social development, as these children are better listeners and interact with their parents, leading to enhanced learning and experience. On the other hand, an uncooperative, insecurely attached child may fail to teach or help parents and eventually may even deter parents from trying to help the baby.

The best way to understand the significance of attachment formation might be to consider the results where it has been obstructed or impeded. Several studies have shown the adverse impact of attachment deprivation on social development–rhesus monkeys were isolated at birth and deprived of any social and environmental stimulation. These monkeys show severe developmental deficits and withdrawal when placed in free play sessions with other people.

The developmental effects of institutionalization were based on similar research with human children (for example, in Romanian orphanages). It was shown that these children are more withdrawn, seldom approach adults, or seek reassurance if in distress. These children are also more vigilant and, therefore, more alarming in school than children raised in their home environment. Yet' healthy' social parenting at an early age is associated with children's behavioral problems and adult personality problems. In the forming process of their personality development, the lack of a stable attachment figure seems to bother these children.

There is a growing research that suggests that depressed people can benefit from early counseling and social care. There have been significant developmental outcomes in children previously without a secure attachment when affectionate and attentive caregivers were added. Parenting courses that concentrate on emotion and connection can also help. Improvements and clear signals of acceptance in the emotional and physical setting will help the child progress towards a more positive sense of self and others. The quality of attachments formed may be altered in improvements in family circumstances and parent-child relationships (e.g., reduction of family pressure, increased social support)

Children who have been abused or other types of childhood abuse are prone to vulnerability. Often issues with parental mental health (including opioid use and substance abuse) are significant precipitating factors. On other occasions, family stress, domestic violence, and a lack of adequate social assistance for parents may be the result. Helping children and families in stable, safe, and healthy environments are in our best interests. There are charitable and statutory support services that work hard to make this aim come true. For further details, please contact me or visit my website.

PASSION AND PURPOSE AS A WAY TO A BETTER LIFE OF KINDNESS

How often do we wonder what we're doing on earth here? What does this ride mean, and what is my role in this enormous cosmic system? When you wake up in the morning and start your new day, do you feel a sense of purpose and meaning in your life? Once you retire at night, do you feel you have made a contribution that makes you feel confident with what you put on today's mainstream life?

However, these questions we ask are an essential part of our lifetime and journey. So many people are unconscious, unconnected, addicted, and clueless about what their intention is to be here. While I, Bob, was at college, I had the opportunity to work in a small schoolhouse as a way of earning college credit for children with special needs. In the 1960s, during the' Tune in, Turn on, and Drop Out' period, and with no shortage of' Altered State ' experiences, my college years had the privilege of working with these people.

Looking at the work you do and the roles you perform as a parent, spouse, community member, son, and daughter, it is easy to realize that some services are woven into all these different roles. They are designed to give and serve naturally. There are tasks for each of us, there's a lot, and no escape. Therefore, if we live from a new paradigm, we miss the boat about what our motivation and mission are. Obstacles fall; actions that are self-defeat and valuable hinder your ability to fulfill your goal and your desires. Each one has elements of fear that isolate us from our authenticity.

Our first obstacle is the "Pleasing Others" Syndrome (also known as co-dependence). If there is a predisposition in your job/service experience to seek approval and think endlessly about satisfying others, this emphasis is in the way of happiness and pleasure surrounding your work, and this generates a strain and weight when the main motive is to seek validation. A huge amount of fear and insecurity is rooted in this process.

This fear can take hold of you in such a way that your success and acceptance ratings generate increasing anxiety and therefore deprive you of the dopamine response (natural opioids in the brain) released from a position of validity. The more you unlock and explore your fears, the more you gravitate to the Love and Intent waiting to show itself.

When we talk about fears, it's about self-deception, several shortcomings, and prejudices that hamper the grandeur. There are, of course, healthy worries that keep you safe and secure. Such worries are built into our brains so that we don't get hurt. The trick is to discern when our healthy fear mechanisms are triggered versus a misguided belief in the need for continuous approval or affirmation.

The second impediment to living in place of Passion and Objection is the attitude and behaviors which suggest that you must be "the Superstar." Once, paranoia will be at the center of this philosophy from which you work. Those kinds of vulnerability become very rewarding when you work from a position of goodness, compassion, and empathy.

Operating arrogantly (I'm not wrong) leaves you without modesty, which is an integral part of the satisfaction of passion and intention. We must be willing and able to forgive our mistakes and make mistakes as long as we work sincerely for the greater good that we serve. You are living in a state of Love and Intent if you can honestly say that you gave yourself for fun and for free, without the need for incentives or recognition.

The third stumbling block in the way you live from a genuine passion and intent is to exclude the spirit from the process. Passion and intent carry a creative and satisfying strength. You can feel tired as a result of the work you have done, but to the same degree, you experience motivation as a result of the creative process.

People were taught in the corporate world to take their souls out of the calculation. If we don't carry our soul to work, then climbing the ladder or creating a business success is a hollow activity that encourages you to push, press, and drive to achieve what we call joy and fulfillment. It is pure joy and satisfaction to put our mind and soul to work.

Perfectionism is the fourth challenge to achieving Love and Intent. The perfectionist demands unrealistically himself and others. It will profoundly hinder the pursuit of happiness and create a barrier to the fulfillment of your purpose and ambition if you are committed to always being right, rendering others wrong.

We can all strive for excellence without governing, manipulating, and judging ourselves. The lack of compassion, kindness, and empathy once again lies at the heart of perfectionism and fear is rooted in the heart. If you live from a sensitive and controlled location, the unexpected answer to challenges induces defensiveness. As a consequence, even if you are correct, there will be disconnection and alienation.

All the obstacles and falls mentioned above are based on fear. A framework of selfishness and self-centeredness is built out of fear. These mistakes are so ingrained into our work culture that they are considered normal. Thankfully, more and more of us are waking to the need to improve and to find ways to serve others.

Natural law will always work for us if we fulfill our passion and purpose. Following your call, there will only be people, resources, and support systems. You're no different than a lighthouse with its light that shows the way to the ships on the sea. The quality of life within each one of us is fundamental to our sincerity and, therefore, our innovation. If we linked to this deep place within, we can escape fear and attract all the good we can ever imagine.

Below are a couple of questions you have to ask for your passion and intent.

1. What excites you enough that you want to play with it every day?
2. Do time and space temporarily cease to exist when you do this exciting thing?
3. Were you mentally, emotionally, and spiritually challenged?
4. Are these difficulties a sense of achievement, satisfaction, and success?
5. If you engage in what excites you, do you have a clear sense that you want to do that?
6. Do you like this work so much that you would do it free of charge?
7. Do you get excited about what you do when you talk to others?

If you can answer all these questions, yes, you certainly live in a place of love and intention. If you wake up to your job without the enthusiasm, imagination, and excitement that go with it, please allow others to help you. You enjoy feeling fulfilled in the above lifetime and to look down and feel that you have changed for the better of humanity and the world.

3 Keys to a Fit and Happy Life

We can all go on and on, of course, but you get the idea. The message that I would love to extract from this chapter is to learn to grow, use, and express appreciation. Gratitude is something we need to stop thinking about ourselves and start to appreciate something or someone else. We learn courage from it, we learn selflessness, we learn humility, and we know that our thought, acts, and purpose always matter meaning spirited thoughts, deceptive transactions, and envy generate unhappiness, suffering, and indulgence. Through time, this produces, develops, and strengthens our problems thereby increasing our unhappiness, and consolidates our negativity.

Here are three ways to foster an appreciation and to feel better. I hope you're going to try them.

1. Stop being lazy and think of it.

Yes, it sounds simple, but how many times in the day do you stop and are actively seeking to thank aspects of your life? What about your boss, children, animals, family, and your job? What about your work? All these things can easily be moved from positive to negative thoughts, depending on how we interact with them.

Your children need so much time and effort, but that's why you aspire for change. You want a better life for them than you had. Thank you for them.

Your job fails, you have trouble meeting deadlines, and your daily schedule is not under your power. However, it also pays for the bills, and it ensures that you have a pleasant place to live, and you can enjoy all your activities and events. Even if your job sucks, be thankful while you're looking for another.

There are countless examples of things or people who can add to our workload and tension. Take a moment to thank them while you are working to improve this situation.

2. Keep a gratitude calendar.

Sometimes, we have to remember things and people we have to thank. We use a calendar to structure our lives. It's also one of the most important ways to ensure that your thanks are always at the forefront of your mind.

Before every month starts, take a few minutes to think about the things and people that give you pleasure, motivation, and gratitude at the moment. During every day you may be thankful for these things, make sure you set aside a special day to give meaningful thanks to these things and people, so they know what they mean to you. Even if you cannot tell the people, try to find a way to make them know that they're important to you.

The great Wallace D. Wattles once wrote that gratitude brings us to the root of our blessings. I think this is true. We can't distance ourselves from frustrated thinking without appreciation. Gratitude will take your thoughts and intentions and put them to work for you to draw closer to you, the things and people you need. Life is important. Learn to say thanks and watch your life change in a positive way that you could never have imagined.

3. Enter, Compete, Try!

I sometimes consider people who lead very mundane lives out of fear of failure. We have little to be happy and enthusiastic about because they have never done anything that they deem deserving of praise. Their fear of failure and embarrassment prevents them from doing things of the kind that could best accomplish them. There are many great ways to achieve this today, especially in terms of diet and exercise, without fear of failure. There were so many highly competitive competitions for those who want to participate. For example, almost every running event, I think, is mainly full of people who want to cross the finishing line, but they never cross it first. Such people want success, personal growth, and the sense that they have achieved something fantastic! Try to find ways to push yourself and do it! A 5k, 10k, or marathon train. Join a local club and participate in events that allow you to train hard, compete, and do more than you dreamed. Remember, for most of us, improving doesn't mean to be the best but to be the best we can be today, and this is a pretty good sensation and is available to anyone who takes the time to pursue their dreams and improve with a strong sense of gratitude.

CHAPTER TWO

ATTACHMENT THEORY FOR ADULTS AND COUPLES

The theory of attachments may be studied and dissected in several ways but is described as a way of demonstrating the dynamics of interpersonal relationships among humans in its simplest form, and this can begin with relationships between parents and children, friendships, and romantic relationships. Usually, four sides of attachment theory are used by most models to describe it: free, worried, dissident, and terrifying.

For example, when your parent comes into the room in childhood, a healthy child might wave or say a simple greeting. A concerned child would hardly acknowledge their presence, find other things more enticing, choose to neglect them intentionally, and a frightful child would cling to the parent, deeply afraid of leaving or even not loving enough.

How can romantic relations be affected?

These rules of attachment can certainly lead to adulthood and affect our relations with our families and friends. The attachment theory is a psychological paradigm, so the theories behind it come from a combination of childhood education and predetermined psychological thought that a child does not matter. Naturally, this means that it can be difficult even as an adult to get rid of these feelings.

Based on the' hand' of a person's attachment, it may cause problems in their daily relationships if they do not learn to resolve it.

The attachment theory is similar to childhood relationships between a child and its parent in adult relations. Sadly, these qualities may be considered extremely dangerous, depending on how deeply rooted the problems are in a certain individual.

Similar to the ways of a child's attachment, a person may encounter several attachment problems where his or her partner basically' replaces' the parental figure in their lift, and this might range from being rejected in relationships to concerned about other things, or what could be called the worst; a daunting relationship that leads to needs that can never be fulfilled. The frightening side of attachment can lead to paranoia, stress, or even obsession.

When in the relationship itself and the person you are with, whether they be with you 24 hours a day or if you only see each other regularly, the healthiest type of connection in virtually any relationship is secure.

Combating certain types of attachment that could be considered unhealthy, not only in a romantic way but in any adult relationship, can contribute to harmful ties. Luckily, these unsanitary approaches to binding to others are handled with the right therapeutic help and coaching.

ATTACHMENT THEORY AND DEVELOPMENT OF EATING DISORDERS

Attachment theory describes the relation or bond between a child and his/her parent or guardian. It is now becoming clear that children with an unstable relationship are more vulnerable to eating disorders than children with healthy attachments.

As children communicate with parents during their first 5-7 years, some children feel that their parents are a reliable source of security and comfort. Such children are most likely to become stable and well-adjusted adults.

Additional children that feel that their parents (or caregivers) are not so trustworthy and do not give them a sense of protection, encouragement, and comfort when required. Some parents may even refuse to offer emotional comfort to their children. Such children will probably develop an unhealthy attachment style and compensate for emotional discomfort as they grow up with food, alcohol, and drugs.

Already we know that many patients with anorexia, bulimia, and binge eating resort to food abuse to find safety, security, and emotional stability. Food is something that is often readily available and provides a patient with immediate emotional comfort: it, therefore, seems an easy way out of emotions.

Parents are not to blame because eating disorders are complex, and a person's illness needs multiple causes to come together. Yet what we now know is that a cold upbringing, high expectations on a child, neglect or rejection by parents are all factors that can lead a child to a food disorder.

Most people with anorexia, bulimia, and binge eating (almost all) usually have nervous styles: depressed or avoidable because of attachment types formed in the first years of life, it is understandable that eating disorder predisposition is established in the previous lifetime (probably in the first 5-7 years of life).

A child's attitude towards its parents (caregivers) is also directly related to his/her attitude towards himself/herself, body and self-esteem, his/her environment, and his/her people. It is also related to their sense of protection (or not a safe place in the world). All these factors, as we know now, affect the development of food disorders in young children and adolescents.

Finally, we should look at attachment style when learning about the prevention of eating disorders. They will teach parents how to make their children feel safer and more comfortable with themselves. Developing a healthy type of attachment in children is going to help many young people avoid eating disorders.

ATTACHMENT THEORY AND THE ORIGINS OF SHAME

Without a doubt, you know the nature vs. sustainability debate about the relative importance of heredity and the environment. Today, the prevalent view seems to be that it is not either one or the other that defines us, but rather the interaction between them. Yet, most people believe that you are born into the world with your entire genetic makeup and connect with your surroundings. In his YouTube video on Attachment Theory, Allan Schore, a member of the Faculty of Psychiatry and Comportment at University of Colombia (UCLA) contradicts this view: "One of the great misconceptions many scientists have is that all that is before birth is hereditary and everything that is learned after birth." That's not so. "Primitive brain" or "Only the brain stem is well developed," the remaining brain develops and evolves for the next two years, as neurons are myelinated and interconnected. This growth is not inevitable and predetermined in all people; in particular, experiences and relationships with primary guardians are influenced by the environment.

It's a more nuanced view of the argument between nature and nurture. It is not only nature and feeding, as most of us already believe; in the first two years of life, the particular genetic makeup (nature) of a single person often evolves under the influence of the environment (food). In other words, mentally and physically, during the first two years–and in particular the first nine months– your neurological development will be strongly influenced and decided how your brain stays in shape. The most significant parts of the brain that develop during these early months are "the child's emotional and social functioning." And if such parts of the brain are to develop "other interactions properly are needed, which are part of the relationship between the child-caregiver and the child." In this critical period, when the organism does not receive sufficient stimuli, it can never evolve those functions or only in very difficult or restricted ways.

So what did Schore say to us? In his opinion, if a baby does not receive emotional stimuli from the parents in the early months of his life, his/her brain will not grow optimally. Instead, some neurons that should have been interconnected die. 'Use or lose'— if in those first two years you don't get what you need, the experience will change you for life. As my client translates it, it means "brain injury." You may be able to change this damage to a certain degree with a lot of hard work, but you'll never be the person you could have been if you had what you need during this critical period.

Profoundly sober thinking. You may call it what you want-bad parenting, failure to adapt, and unhealthy attachment, but in the first two years in life when it goes wrong between the parent and the child, and you get permanently damaged of ways that cannot be removed. The realization that you are impaired and the sense that you have not been able to do what you need and that your mental growth has been deeply skewed— this is what I call simple disgrace.

Schore's view shows that this simplistic view of mental disease as a chemical imbalance in the brain is ridiculous. You do not lack sufficient serotonin in your neural synapses; rather, during the first two years of life, the presence or lack of specific neurons and the interconnections between them were continuously altered by attachment failures. You can't fix a drug for that. Of course, affirmations and other forms of positive psychology will have little effect on brain damage. Cognitive-behavioral therapy can teach you some useful strategies for managing your trauma, but it will not turn you into another human. Whatever you do, you never will be like the person who witnessed the experiences she needs during this critical period.

During this critical period, two other lecturers in this video combine the experience of secure attachment with the creation of a fundamental sense of self-esteem and the capacity to feel empathy towards others. The references to guilt and narcissism are tacit. Either you get what it takes from your caretakers in these early months, and your brain grows in a way that gives you a simple sense of confidence and protection in the world, or you don't get what you need and the result–the neurological harm–is a fundamental shame. If your loved ones are emotionally tuned to you, and you grow (neurological) the capacity to sympathize with other people; or they leave you behind, and your constant fight for a sense of value and significance reduces your ability to sympathize with other people strongly.

At the end of the video, Schore emphasizes the importance of happiness in the attachment experience-i.e. the child's attunement to her mother is vital for the maximum development in the experience of her joy and interest in the infant. If you don't have this experience, if you don't feel your mother's joy and loveliness in your presence, it will permanently damage your mind when it develops. The baby whose mother doesn't love it (feel a deep joy and interest in it) can never get over it, because its brain's neural development has constantly changed, weakened—because of its inability, during the first year, to find what was needed.

FEELINGS AND ATTACHMENTS

While feelings and emotions are related to human beings, they are explicitly associated with women. Women's feelings and emotions are apparent either by their connection to human beings or to worldly things. It is the inherent nature of women, and it is also challenging and important.

The definition and the structural meaning of the concept are important, and the same must be understood and evaluated. A sensation, the term was first used in English to describe the physical feeling of touch by experience or perception. It is also used to describe sensations other than the actual sensation of touch, such as a warmth feeling. For psychology, the word is used for the perception of emotion.

Nature provides and demonstrates happiness and joy in a human being's daily life. Nevertheless, human behavior conditions and prevalent situations test it, with few exceptions. These are predetermined and tested to measure the actions of human beings in various circumstances, and this displays emotions and feelings of sadness and anguish. The actions and actions of people, therefore, clearly reflect the feelings and emotions of joy and sorrow.

Women are physiologically frail, vulnerable, and socially gullible. She expresses her feelings and emotions easily and needs a shoulder to cry or share with someone compassionate to her. At this crucial point, she connects herself to reliable people and expresses her feelings and emotions. It is now interesting and fascinating to look at the complexities of connection.

Attachment is a special emotional relationship that involves an exchange of comfort, care, and pleasure. The origins of attachment studies started with Freud's love theories. Nevertheless, John Bowlby's theory of attachment (An English psychiatrist) is the foundation of attachment among adults, and this is based on the assumption that the foundation is secure. It is well known that the' Attachment Theory' explains the complexities of long-term human relations. This relationship builds on mutual trust, common behaviors, and joint thoughts at a level of acceptable standards. Such relationships are directly proportional to individual attachments.

Study the areas of human relationships which deeply defines attachments. It is also a reality that emotions and feelings depend primarily on attachments. Therefore, the theory of attachment clearly shows human nature and behavior. In the late 1980s, the theory of attachment was applied to adult-romantic relations. There were four forms of attachments found in adults: stable, anxious-preoccupied, dismissive-avoidant, and frightening-avoidant.

In intimate adult affairs, Cindy Hazan and Phillip Shaver applied attachment theory. They realized that interactions between grown-up loving partners share similarities with children's interactions with caregivers. The origins of emotions and attachments are directly linked to human behavior. The sense of belonging indicates that love and affection build strong human relationships, and women play an important role.

The emphasis of all attachments, therefore, revolves around her personality. The effect on your relationship also depends on your participation. The possessive qualities and not the feeling and commitment of her partner to others are dominant in her attitude. It is her stubbornness that governs her senses. The' I ' aspect also contributes to a debacle in her personality. Her thoughts thus outweigh the emotions and attachments of other individuals.

Practically, all-wise, men use sense and sensitivity to provide women with warmth. They also express their peripheral feelings, emotions, and attachments to her. Their behavior balances their actions and keeps them harmonious. When women ignore signs such as pain and fractures form in a healthy relationship or otherwise. The Indian film producer, director, and actor of ancient times, the humorous dimension of women's personality. He said,

"She supposes and opposes." While sentiments, emotions, and attachments have their impact, however, using sensibilities would maintain a delicate balance without jeopardizing its structure.

CHAPTER THREE

THE PSYCHOLOGY OF CHILDREN

Child psychology is related to the personal and social development of kids, and a kid goes through several phases before reaching the adult world following developmental theories on the full psychology of children. The psychology of children has been studied from different angles, including questions of biology and nutrition; whether the infant is a result of genes and ancestry or a product of culture and environment; as well as various stages in the development of sensory tolerance, cognition, emotional and learning through language and cognitive evolution; mental and educational growth. The study of infant sexuality and sexual and moral growth is also particularly important from a psychoanalytical point of view.

Children are vulnerable and easily impacted by all immediate events. Things that are insignificant or meaningless to adults only can leave deep scars or memories in the mind of a child. A child's mind is extremely impressible and changeable, and certain very insignificant events can have great personal importance in a child's life before the child reaches adolescence. Thus "infantile memories" and "infantile events" are primary factors for determining patterns of adult personality. Some important factors that can affect a child's future development and possibly have long-term effects are

1. Friend loss or gain
2. Memorable body / physical emotions
3. Community split or parent divorce
4. Domestic abuse or misconduct
5. Sexual abuse or molestation
6. Learning experiences at practice or study

7. Personal events that evoked strong feelings of fear, joy, sorrow, and so on
8. Accidents or diseases observed or experienced
9. Death of relatives, neighbors, or neighbors
10. Residence change or relocation
11. Friends, teachers, or family
12. Emotional relationships.
13. Individual school success or failure
14. Films, films, books, or news events affect fighting, terrorism, war, bombing, etc.

The factors here are very common, and every child undergoes certain very specific events that affect him or her personally, although certain very general theories are developed in psychology through study, and the theories have highlighted the connection between success or failure in his or her later life and childhood eve. Lev Vygotsky is some of the main children's development theorists. While Bowlby stressed the bond between children, Piaget concentrated on children's cognitive development across various phases, and Freud wrote extensively about kid's sexual growth. Kohlberg studied child moral development, while Vygotsky studied child socialization through social contextualism. All these hypotheses on various aspects of child development show only the enormous complexity and the varying number of factors that play a role in children's psychological development. The psychology of children varies from social, physical, cognitive, sexual, and moral. Here is a brief account of all those theories and comprehensive analysis of how these theories can be used, together with the general factors above mentioned in the study of children's psychology.

The' attachment theory' was developed by John Bowlby, a British psychiatrist who stressed the importance of a mother or a primary career in the lives of a child. In his research, he showed that every child should develop and maintain a warm and intimate relationship with the mother and that any motherly neglect may lead to serious problems in the child's mental health later in life. Bowlby's theory is true, and a mother should build a strong physical and emotional intimacy with the child at least until the child is two years old. Doctors around the world have suggested breastfeeding, and the physical closeness between the child and the mother is a major element of this, which is necessary once the child has left the womb of the mother. The first emotion is fear, when the infant is released from the womb of the mother, and the continued physical closeness of the mother inspires a sense of confidence and comfort in the child. Orphaned children or children separated at birth from their mothers require a substitute for themselves, or they may grow up as mentally ill or disadvantaged persons.

Provided a complete psychosexual theory that emphasizes the sexual pleasure of children, which many of us do not like to believe. Freud overturned the idea of childhood innocence and proposed that we come into being with our unrepressed fundamental impulses, gradually tempered by social adaptation. Freud claims that there are different stages of psychosexual development inherent in the desire that we are born with an emphasis on some erogenous areas of the body, beginning with the vaginal, anal, phallic, latent, and genital levels. Through psychosexual development, the gratification of finding behavior changes from the mouth as when you sucked and bit during toilet training and then finally to the genitals. Therefore, the kid receives complete sexual gratification from psychoanalysis by sucking, scratching, playing with the genitals, and releasing defecation waste. I do not necessarily support Freud's theories on children's sexual pleasure, and the enjoyment of their physical sensations could be clarified differently, as I shall address in another post.

The French-Swiss philosopher Jean Piaget established the theory of child cognitive development, setting forth four-stage development-the sensor motor stage, the pre-operational stage, the concrete stage of operation, and the formal stage of operations. The first stage is when the child develops spatial skills and gets to know the world through the senses in the first two years of life. The second stage includes learning and using ideas as children understand the meaning of things, and it goes on until they are 7. The child reaches higher cognitive growth from 7-11 years through specific organizational stages and can sort, distinguish objects, and use reasoning to solve problems. The formal stage of activity that starts around the age of 12 helps children understand abstract thoughts, hidden meanings, etc. Kohlberg presented a theory of children's moral development across six phases at the pre-conventional, traditional, and post-conventional stages. They include retribution and self-interest and the need to adapt and work for social order, as well as the enforcement of basic ethical principles. Thus moral development appears to move from the belief in' what's good and what's wrong' and whether the wrong is punished by universally ethical and acceptable social behavior. Another prominent psychologist Vygotsky emphasized the importance of socialization and interpersonal communication and the development of children, according to which social and cultural knowledge is seen as an internalization.

Of course, all these hypotheses have to be applied, and there will be a complete or full hypothesis that gives an insight into the mind and actions of the infant that incorporates all these theories. Also, childhood experiences and events highlighted in psychoanalytic theories are extremely important, not simply from a sexual perspective. All of the general factors I mentioned at the beginning of this essay should be seen as factors that underlie children's social, sexual, moral, emotional, physical, and cognitive development while learning experiences contribute to cognitive development, the subsequent emotional development, and awareness of personal emotional experience. Sexual abuse or other forms of childhood bodily sensation may affect subsequent sexual development, and divorce or family breakup may affect morality. A person who has been distressed as a child can either develop a fear of sexual activity or can show an increasing lack of sexual restriction as an adult.

A kid who lived without a dad can either be extremely irresponsible or become an adult who has a strong sense of parental responsibility. Natural calamities have a profound influence on children, enduring childhood trauma through death or injuries of family members or living in wartime may leave a permanent sense of insecurities or of an attachment in the child that persists into adulthood and even old age or, on the other hand, make a child alienated, schizophrenic or disconnected in later life. In a healthy child's life, it is necessary not only to rely on psychological theories for understanding how a child develops and understands the world but also to concentrate on the children's events or experiences and apply them together with children's theories to fully understand their psychology.

Within contemporary child psychology, events are primarily psychoanalytic and especially important are the effects of adverse events. Nevertheless, all events, both positive and negative, should be considered and used to support psychological theories. To understand the child, it is important to understand the context and memories of the child to equalize children's "event-based" psychology with children's "theory-based" psychology.

"Attachment parenting" is a phrase developed by Dr. William Sears, who described such a parenting method based on the fundamental points of attachment theory. By the attachment theory, there is a strong emotional connection in early childhood between the child and the mother, dad and guardian. The idea is based on people's wish to have relationships with others, and it is thought that children will benefit from safe and steady interactions with their fathers and mothers, which will then catalyze empathic connections in the future lives of younger people.

In the last six decades, psychologists, child development professionals, and brain researchers have dealt with the hypotheses and methods of attachment parenting thoroughly. All their findings have pointed to one particular aspect: the brain of the baby is' hard-wired' and an intense need to be nurtured by an emotionally close primary caregiver.

There are several basic principles on attachment parenting that have evolved around its original concept. The first rule is that the mother is ready for conception and the arrival of the infant into the world. When the mom understands what will happen, she will be able to set realistic expectations for herself and her husband.

The second rule is that the infant should have the best possible food options. Although breastfeeding is the best approach to meet the neurological and nutritional requirements of a child, feeding the baby from a bottle can also help to create a safe link. Learning the signs to give babies and children what they need allows them to learn how to eat when they are hungry and know when they are full.

Neurological functions of babies are still not fully developed after they enter the world, and they will need the help of patients and the understanding of fathers and mothers to ease themselves or suffer distress. The proper response to an injured, hungry, or distressed newborn or young person will help them know how to relax as they mature and develop. Also, snoring, listening, and sucking by babies are early techniques they use to keep their father or mother or guardian close to each other. As newborns fulfill their primary needs, cognitive preferences and physiological changes increase. When young people get older and have greater confidence in their ties with their parents, they can check their atmosphere and create great connections with people.

Evenings also offer many ways to communicate securely with a child. Newborns also have night specifications, as they do during the day. Using several of the most common sleep training can damage a child's subsequent growth. Remember that young children can also exploit their environment well, so that dads and moms are sensitive and compassionate to address the needs of the infant while being strong if these nighttime outbursts are more of a ritual than a necessity.

Newborns need steady guidance, particularly from a mother or father. If another guardian is required, then seek to slowly introduce the newborn guardian so that there is a bond between them. Ensure good discipline among all guardians. An important rule of attachment parenting is that mother or father offers positive discipline. It ensures that training is used in a moist and empathic way that respects the weak points and strengths of a little one. While children should not be punished, little children call for open communication lines and guidance to help them change their actions and protect the integrity of all.

Another concept of parenthood is the preservation of a healthy personal and family life for mothers and fathers. If the adult feels happy and emotionally fed, it is less difficult to respond to a newborn or a youngster emotionally. Some strategies for this are the supportive network of close friends, the formation of specific goals for both the father and mother and the entire family unit, and the ability to say no if work responsibilities compromise the ability of adults to care for their loved ones.

Such ideals are interpreted in several ways by fathers and mothers; some include natural birth, home birth, co-sleeping, natural health and well-being, home schools, or organic foods, which fall within the framework of those concepts. Bear in mind, however, that these are rules which help dads and moms realize how emotional attachment to their young can help them to improve their ability to become mature people and not only rationalize behavior.

PARENTING THE ATTACHMENT CHALLENGED CHILD

There's a lot of literature these days about how parents pressure children. However, many of this literature generally does not discuss the child with specific parenting needs and a different understanding of the environment. A child diagnosed with reactive attachment disorder, oppositional defiant disorder, or even depression does not need to understand the conduct, but rather the underlying dynamics that drive behavior. Take, for example, the iceberg analogy. Usually, we refer to what we see above the water when we refer to an iceberg.

Nevertheless, 90% of all icebergs are invisible and lie under the surface. What you think is an iceberg is just the tip. It's a daunting thought in the light of how big an iceberg is above the sea. Picture the other 90% lurking below.

Negative children's behaviors are much the same. While we can try to remove an iceberg by hacking down the top, we will spend an endless amount of time and energy concentrating on the smallest aspect of the iceberg. When parents are motivated to focus on reducing actions only through simplistic behavior modification models, boot camp strategies, or rational outcomes, the most important part of the action is lacking. Concentrating only on the behavior will usually eradicate the behavior for a while to see only another day return with greater intensity. Specific parenting strategies should be taken to help reduce problem behavior effectively over a short period. The steps will not be easy to follow, although the effectiveness of each approach is guaranteed to be effective with a firm determination to remain on track.

The stress Model

This plays a vital role in all we do. We depend on stress to stay alive and engage the outside world as an internal experience. We often rely on stress to fight illness, digest food, and recover from times of difficulty.

Just laughing is a state of stress. They are dependent on a theory of human behavior called the stress model when evaluating parenting strategies for traumatic behavior. The stress model is a very simple behavioral theory which says, "ALL behavior arises out of a stressful situation and between behavior and stress is the presence of one of the two main emotions: Love or Fear, which can calm down the stress and reduce the behavior through expression, processing, and comprehension of the emotion."

Really important point: only two primary emotions are present–love and fear.

Wrath is not an emotion. It is a sensation secondary to the body's terror. Experience of fear can occur on any sensory path. You see, hear, touch, smell, taste, and even your body temperature. Stress and fear are experienced cellularly, and this happens unconsciously. You're not always going to know what triggers anxiety or tension. If you see rage, wrath, envy, and more, it comes from fear, not from hatred. The gap between the two people is passion. It is always around us every day. Our fear is the only thing that keeps us out of love. Because the presence of love is inevitable, we are responsible for putting fear aside and entering the presence of love. You might have listened to it, saying, "Perfect love casts out all fear," or, "Love and fear cannot coexist." What we confidently interpret as love is nothing more than fear in disguise.

More often than not, we don't see this because most of the time, we don't see our terror. It is important to remember the fear and stress they cause in a parent when thinking about the particular, extreme behaviors. When you attempt to overcome fear by generating more fear, you raise fear.

WHAT YOU NEED TO KNOW ABOUT ATTACHMENT PARENTING TOOLS

A term called attachment parenting was coined. It is a parenting philosophy that is based on the principles of the developmental psychology of attachment theory. It's also called stable attachment, where one is in a strong emotional bond with parents, when one reaches adulthood; it becomes the foundation for a healthy emotional relationship.

Based on the theory of attachment, parenting of attachment is established. The theory gives us an idea that the infant or child wants to interact closely with a parent and feel the comfort and affection when they are there. In the theory of attachment, the child is attached because it involves human beings, and human beings are social persons. They are not attached because they need another adult to meet their needs for love and connection that is a natural part of the development of a child.

“Seven Bs” is the bonding device Dr. Sears tends to show the babies the best by adding some loving style. The seven Bs include birth bonding, lactation, baby wearing, bedding close to the infant, confidence in your child's scream, and baby trainers ' language interest.

Another reminder that Dr. Sears gives the parents is that attachment parenting is a starter style and that other factors may preclude parents from practicing “seven Bs.” It should be kept in mind that the “seven Bs” are not considered rigid guidelines where the signs and level of need of the child are to be accepted, understood, acknowledged, and responded to, whether in medical, environmental, or family circumstances.

AP (attachment parenting) is also emphasized as a tool and not as a step. A technique can be diversified and independently applied based on what is useful and applicable where strict preparation in a single step is required, and the failure to perform one process makes the entire scene a mess. The final reminder Dr. Sears gave was to stick to what works for them and to adjust the tolls. Parenting styles provide an avenue for design and help both parents and children to create a healthy and loving attachment.

CHAPTER FOUR

UNDERSTANDING THE RULES CONTROLLING YOUR LIFE

You must be in control of your life. It describes the way you feel effective in your life. What you and I call daily life at this age is very different from what our grandparents and even our parents called everyday life. All now feels so much more complicated than ever.

The more we grow, the more we learn about ourselves and repress the restrictions of what we can achieve in human species. Likewise, as you grow older and gain a better understanding of the world in which you live, you too change complexity.

Have you ever found that, with all the latest developments in science and technology, the human race has not advanced much on the psychological side of things? This disparity can also be seen at an individual level in social growth verses.

You are blessed with the constant and endless desire to explore and learn something new. Once you learn something new, the mind is at its best. I know you can remember a time when you were very nervous about new things; something you thought at first was complicated. Time and practice made it easier for you to do this job without thinking one day.

Maybe it was like learning how to drive, you faced learning new things and had to learn the rules to master driving. What did you do? What did you do? You could go out and buy any book you could find on driving and heartily learn the rules. But that wouldn't have qualified you to drive a car.

It was when you wanted to do something new and save on driving with a trainer that you began learning how to apply and to understand the rules of driving.

This approach extends to most new situations in your life and future. To understand something, you must learn the rules first. Then you have to follow these rules and learn them for yourself and see the results to master the subject. The more you follow the basic rules, the happier you are, and soon after you master the basics, you will be taught more complicated things like positioning your vehicle, etc. Ideally, you have enough experiences before you learn the basics of a certain area of your life to move on to complicated things. You are therefore trying to achieve your goals without taking the time to figure out what you need to do first to get there before you have understood what you want and why in your life.

One example is the classic story of a child walking through the forest and being surprised by a butterfly that flies out of the bushes they scare as they pass across the wood. The feeling is so overwhelming, and without proper analysis, it is locked as terror into the subconscious. So when the child grows up because they have not learned any other laws, they are scared of butterflies and moths.

This example can be used to describe any experience in your life where things did not go well, and you felt terrified. Examinations, work interviews, first seeing the person you dream, and don't know how to tell them. You know someone who has if you haven't done it. Learning to identify certain patterns of reactions in your life will help you to create new and eternal positive life changes.

Just imagine a typical reaction with me when you come into contact with a specific situation that pushes you beyond your comfort zone. How are you feeling inside? Are you feeling helpless? How would you like to behave if you look back on the situation?

You see, these are all laws you have developed to help you deal with the variety of things you felt threatened. Once you have heard, they are placed in your unconscious mind to immediately follow that path and prevent the perceived danger the next time you feel this.

In general, the rules you apply to your life are designed to protect you from possible physical or mental damage. It is the innate desire to move away from pain and to enjoy. You can learn different things by repeating and reasoning. Once your emotions are involved, the whole rational higher intellect-conscious cycle is destroyed, and your impulses are taken over because your brain can not differentiate between the danger of mortal life and the suffering that you feel in emotional situations. The main task is to get you away from pain and protection and, if you are unable to escape a safer place, at the very least, to defend yourself through some reaction.

In such a scenario, you have people who say things like, "I feel bad when he looks at me," or "being late means you don't care for me."

There are many reasons why you do what you do in certain cases. The intention is not to erase but to consider your emotions. Building on your beliefs and values with a personal coach lets you focus on things that do not serve you well in your lives. You are better equipped by knowing them to deal with the things you want in your life. A life coach is a professional in creating an environment that helps you to concentrate on yourselves and to answer all the questions you dread asking people in your current circle of influence.

LIVING THE ATTACHED LIFE

"Why do you feed it so badly?" says Julia, 33, who heard it repeatedly since her son was born ten months ago. "Babies ought to sleep in their cot," and "you shouldn't carry him so much; you will spoil him." The indicators come from meaningful parents and other self-appointed advisors on the education of children in her circle.

Since Julia is very often breastfeeding, she often holds her baby on demand, and she lets him sleep in a bed curled next to her daughter, and even on her tummy sometimes. And all of this is because she does not doubt in mind that it is best for her and her baby, to raise her child following her intuition and common sense.

And Julia's not alone. Indeed, women in most parts of the world still raise their babies every day by meeting their immediate needs, carrying and wearing, and sleeping with them, and most of all, because they live in less modern cultures, without any access to pushchairs, baby cabins, and child-raising literature just as our ancestors have done since days started.

In our modernized world, however, parents can choose how to raise their children. We did and tried all from placing children to sleep on their bellies to let them "cry" out because they were told to do so, with the access to extensive information on childhood education from literature to experts. It's no wonder that parents often become confused about what to believe, particularly since many therapists and pedagogues seem to be changing their mind about the best method of raising children for every new decade and some revolutionizing approaches, which in the past have become a common place and successful, have later been found to harm the mental health of the baby.

It is perhaps why we see a new trend towards returning to a more natural and "traditional" parenting method, which fosters close relationships between baby and mother and this is a child's growing way of keeping faith in Mother Nature's wisdom, and this theory of no foolishness that has worked well for mothers over the centuries was called "The Theory of Attachment" in our contemporary society.

In the 1960s, British psychiatrist and developmental psychologist John Bowlby (1907-1990) coined the term "attachment" when he proposed a theory that builds on a theory of biological bonding between a mother and her child. Bowlby researched children below three who are hospitalized, institutionalized and elsewhere removed from their mothers, and found that the bond between mother and baby is much stronger than before (Bowlby believed at the time that mothers were the primary attachment, but later studies showed children are attached to both parents). In 1958 Bowlby first proposed his theory of attachment, based on ethological principles, and described three different stages of separation between children, suggesting that the more the children are attached to their mother, the less will they be distressed compared to if they are separated from her.

During his later studies, together with others, the attachment theory was further developed, and thanks to the' Strange Situation,' the' laboratory technique for the study of child-parent attachment' developed by Mary Ainsworth and her students, children began to understand formally the individual differences in how the attachment figure is accessible to and how it is controlled.

The "strange scenario" was created in the laboratory where a child was separated, rejoined, and the reaction of the child was observed. Ainsworth identified the individual differences in three key patterns of attachment: the healthy child who was upset when the mother left the room but was easy to console when she returned; the nervous, aggressive children who were extremely upset at separation but had trouble being reassured when she returned and often exhibited contradictory behaviors that wanted comfort but also that wanted to be comforted.

Ainsworth found that such variations were associated with the relationship between child and parent in the home during their first few years; a healthy child had attachment figures that were attentive to his needs, while an anxious, aggressive or avoided child had an attachment figure which is either insensitive and inconsistent or simply inaccessible.

A child with an attachment that provides a safe foundation is playful, adventurous, less inhibited, more smiling, and sociable than a child without a sure mother's attachment, and has also found evidence of the negative developmental effects of the child lacking a mother figure.

The patterns of attachment developed in early childhood lead us throughout our lives and influence our way of dealing with others, especially our romantic relationships, and its theory has evolved into adult relationships.

Today, the modern theory of attachment has developed. Some scholars disagree about the exact way in which attachment theory can contribute to ideal child re-emergence, but generally agree that the mothers (or other attachment figures) should be available for a secure attachment and be able to respond adequately to the needs of the child. A parent may render this loving connection through the wearing of the baby (carrying the baby in a sling or a baby carrier), prolonged breastfeeding and co-sleep, and constant response to the physical and emotional needs of the infant.

Throughout their comprehensive book, Dr. Sears provides practical knowledge on the growth of children in an easy-to-read style and thorough instructions on how to carry out the kind of attachment parenting that suits the family and lifestyle, noting that attachment parenting involves fathers and can also be carried out by other caregivers.

And while full-time working mothers are not ideal in the parenthood world, there are still plenty of ways for a mother to practice parenthood with her child and build a strong bond between them. Sears proposes that the working mother listens to the needs of her child when at home and offers a caring caregiver who can do parental attachment when she is not. A child should be held, brought to, spoken to, but not always by the mother.

Some Parents fear that a tied parenting style will lead to spoiled, challenging, and clinging children, but extensive research otherwise has shown that tied children are more confident, independent, and social towards others. And several research studies show a clear correlation between child and depression poorly cared for, substance use, abuse, and even divorce in later adulthood.

Like any theory, the attachment theory also has its critics, and the most recent critic suggests that demand feeding is the cause of a growing problem with the obesity of children, as advocated by attachment parenting. Nonetheless, this critique was launched recently in a multi-year study conducted by researchers from Texas A&M University. The research ' Parental Time, Position Strain, and Children's Fat Intake' was reported by the USA last June. Department of Agriculture discovered that the more time parents spend with their children, the less likely the child also becomes obese. Conversely, the more time a mother spends with an infant, the more likely the child is to be obese. All mothers and fathers have to be directly involved in the education of their children and be responsible parents who set a good example for their children by their habits.

A LOOK AT BRAIN DEVELOPMENT, BIRTH ORDER, AND ATTACHMENT THEORY MODELING

Some case studies appear to indicate that babies take precedence over caregiver or parent care. Attachment theory predicts better early brain development for those children with near parental bonds, but what happens when a child is neglected, even slightly, or when a new child sibling enters the mother's time.

Okay, we can deduce that the older children are said to feel neglected based on attachment theory, and this could lead to problems if the children are similar together in age and both in the first two years of life. Therefore, hypothetically the first siblings born into this situation would be at risk from attachment problems.

Psychological studies indicate that firstborns in adulthood are most likely more confident or even entrepreneurial. Would you think the problem of attachment plays a role in these observations? It turns out that most researchers agree with my argument.

Nevertheless, the firstborns could be said to be so at great risk because the caregiver has spent time with the infant. So is this ability to produce children who grow up into borderline children and young adults that are self-reliant? Many assume that with this line of inquiry, I am on track.

How can we be so sure that the offspring will better be weaned from the caregiver's attention to defend itself, thereby developing more self-sufficiency, which is perhaps of greater importance for life's success?

If we now take this whole matter one step further, then a baby with the right caregiver in' clinical psychology ' terms is more dependent than an adult without the' best possible caregiver' as defined in the theory of attachment.

But society would be better served if it had no ideal caregiver or at least 12-15 percent. Why? Ten percent of the population in the United States has its own business, and we need leaders in our society. Especially if everything else depends on external sources, the family and the government now, it seems.

ATTACHMENT THEORY: TIPS EVERY NANNY SHOULD KNOW

Treatment for nannies is a significant activity. Nanny care goes beyond regular baby care, and a nanny must therefore, be equipped with skills above and beyond. Although you are not the parent of the children you care for, you will still have a major impact on their growth as you will be an important person and this is why you want to ensure that your experiences with the kids you care for are meaningful that will foster positive and healthy emotional growth in the baby. A kid who is more familiar with these kinds of topics creates not only better care for kids, but also an employee who is more attractive to a family.

What is attachment In Relating to this?

A relationship is a link between two individuals. In 1969 a psychologist named John Bowlby developed the Attachment Theory, which argued that people's relationships early in life would affect the type of person they will become later. Such early life experiences will influence everything about who we are, our personalities, and our relationships. You can understand how important a successful relationship can be with this knowledge. As a kid, you are one of a child's primary caregivers and will thus have a strong impact on your future self.

How can I create a positive relationship as a nanny?

This is an important issue. You want to try to build what Bowlby's theory calls a safe connection. Some factors may help to create this with a child. The child has to feel that perhaps the caregiver is a safe person, and then someone he/she can come to when he/she needs affection and comfort. A person is not smothering at the same time. We allow the child to explore the world and make mistakes sometimes, but if the child needs comfort, he/she is there. Natural reactions in a child would be that the child wants to be close to the caregiver, but does not rely heavily on it. It means being a trustworthy and loving person in the child's life, but not overprotective or overbearing. It is natural for a child to explore and learn about the world. Sometimes the world can be scary and unpleasant, and the child is a parent, or a nanny will seek solace.

You don't have to be a psychological expert to be a great caregiver. It can also improve your skills as a caregiver to know some of the hypotheses about children and development. If you have decided to start a career in childcare, and you have a passion for babies, brushing up your children's education can do wonders for your skills and career.

WHY ATTACHMENT MATTERS IN ADULT RELATIONSHIPS

The relationship between parent and child is defined in Attachment Theory by the parents' ability to respond physically and emotionally to their children. The relationship is described as either safe or insecure based on the parent's ability to create protection and how the child responds to it. A child must depend on his/her parent to believe that the relationship is a haven and that the world is a safe and secure environment. Kids will assume that when they are in need, their parents will be there for them. I don't know many people who argue that this is not the best way to raise all children. Evolutionally, this need for bonding is hard-wired in all species.

We tend not to think about adult relationship attachment, but it's equally important. For adult relationships, commitment is a bit different because it is mutual. A parent does not expect a sense of safety from its child, but a partner looks for this reciprocity (although they don't know it). Adults must also believe that a partnership provides stability and protection so that they have a deeper, more expressed, more coherent, and optimistic sense of themselves and others. The fact that there is a sexual component is another distinction in adult relationships. There again, we see how to secure the sexual relationship between partners is defined by the need for intimacy and protection. "No protection, no sex" is a common refrain in adult intercourse.

This sense of safety and secure attachment are lacking in distressed relations. Isolation, disconnection, or separation from a relationship (whether it is a parent or a spouse) is painful inherently. Emotional disconnection leads to fear and uncertainty for people. The brain reads the action of the partner as "dangerous," and because of our hard drive for survival, we are fighting, fleeing or freezing.

Each behavior causes a partner to react to a reciprocal feedback loop. Around and around, it looks at a few in a negative cycle that can lead to a breakdown of relationships between spouses. The more anxiety and hopelessness are, the more programmed, linear, and emotional and behavioral reactions between the partners are reinforced.

Couples are trapped in negative reactive behavior and misperception feedback loop. Every time a partner fails to respond in a time of great need, a sense of panic and vulnerability develops until a couple can become engaged and protect themselves over time. Such cycles are driven by anger, sorrow, desire, shame, and fear.

Some partners cannot join a negative cycle as profoundly and can easily escape from any process in which they are trapped. Such couples will convey what disturbed or caused them. Partners can control emotional distress through separation and, when reunited, can send strong, assertive signals of their needs. Securely attached couples will trust each other and embrace comfort and confidence. Moments known as hazardous or dangerous can be recognized and handled. Couples should focus on their experience and construct cohesive, coherent relationship narratives.

In a nutshell, stable couples can address a perceived bond break without triggering a negative attack/retirement period. Couples tend to interact more freely and implicitly and also prefer to expose themselves more to their friends. Further attention is paid to other needs and a greater sense of empathy for the partner. Communication is polite, as well as collaborative. In reality, this is "successful dependency," a capacity to feel connected with someone else but to remain self-confident.

GET YOUR MIND RIGHT, BEGIN BUILDING SELF CONFIDENCE

So how do you train for self-confidence building?

Would you lack confidence in yourself? Next, you need to understand the problem and take action to find a solution. First, you have to start educating yourself. It is the phase that endures forever. We must never stop learning to make success.

One important thing to understand is the cycle of building self-confidence. It won't happen overnight, but you can start seeing and enjoying results as soon as you start working regularly. The good news is that building self-confidence is something that a little awareness and continuous effort can easily achieve.

Once you start practicing what you know and develop self-esteem, you will also start creating more achievements in your life. Such successes will intensify the growth of your confidence. The result is a snowball effect that allows you to trust even more quickly than expected. Confidence builds trust! Often, if your self-esteem is proven consistently by the positive results you experience in your life, your doubts are receded and completely dissolved.

The best way to build self-confidence is by taking steps, and the first step should always be to plan for any worthwhile endeavor.

Get Prepared

Get ready to brace yourself, and you have to know clearly where you are and where you want to be. Only then can an effective plan be created to get there. You know where you stand in self-confidence. You know the types of situations that you can comfortably handle and the types of situations with which you have trouble. Think about it for a while and try to understand what your path to self-confidence is right now.

Consider now where you want to be. Imaging is a powerful mental instrument. Visualize yourself doing things that make you uncomfortable at present. When you do so, feel easy, completely relaxed internally as if you had mastered and completed these things hundreds of times. If your mind can think about it, it can. You now have a clear picture of where you are and what you want to do. File or write down these mental images, this is your motivation, and you can come back to them whenever you need it.

Having your mind right

The next step in getting yourself ready is to get into the right thinking. You must assume that your objectives are achievable before you can commit to them fairly. If this is hard for you, try to use clear, rational thinking. When you think rationally about this target, it becomes obvious that you can not only accomplish it but also potentially. Such self-assurance strategies have been tried, tested, and practiced over many years and before you and me by hundreds of thousands of people. Humanity had plenty of time and test cases to figure out what is and what isn't. Rest assured that the information is available and that what you want is indeed possible. Right now, remove all doubts about this. Accept and move on rationally.

Stop Defeating Yourself

Another important part of your thinking is to make sure you stop working against yourself. We tend to take bad habits that perpetuate negative behavior. Make a conscious effort to get rid of your self-destroying feelings and stop telling you something. For one explanation, you call these bad habits "defeating yourself." That's what they're doing! You heard it "think positive" several times, and you will continue to hear it when you ask people who know how to have faith. Stay positive, stay focused, and take action.

Examine and evaluate your strengths rationally.

The best way to start recognizing your strengths is to take some time and think about your whole life. Starting as early as childhood, find memories of every significant accomplishment in your life. I hope no matter who you are that there will be more. Don't play anything down. If you felt good, it's significant. Write it down. Write it down. When you won a 3rd-grade foot race and remember the great feeling that you had afterward, include it. Do you have the job of five people interviewed? Include it. Compile a list. That's something you're always referring to (at least weekly) to remind you that you can succeed. Concentrate on and highlight the most important ones to you.

Analyze your List

Just look at the list and think about the things you are comfortable with and the ones that still make you uncomfortable. Can you see any trends? You will start seeing where your strengths lie. What's the stuff you' do best? Write down these thoughts. We must all be acutely aware of our abilities to accomplish every important goal.

Develop a plan

The development of a tangible and clearly defined plan is an important component of the process. It lets you assess and bear witness to your progress, which reaffirms your belief that your efforts will be successful. You will learn how to rely on a plan and develop strong habits systematically.

The plan should describe your objectives. Start with a brainstorming list of things you can't handle easily, but expect to do in the future with ease. These are your specific objectives. Include any achievements, even those that appear insignificant. For example, when I asked strangers for directions or support, I used to feel a bit awkward. I decided to approach and speak with faith to everybody so that I would add it to my list. Be not afraid to include those who are tough or to request a raise, give a speech to a room with 1000 people, or ask the girl or guy to have dinner through the door. Now arrange them from easiest to the hardest and concentrate on achieving them before moving on.

Every small success will provide you with a measure of increased trust that helps you get to the next level. Every accomplishment is a building block for self-confidence.

This is the "textbook" objective setting.

You will pass through these achievements from simplest to harshest over time, and each time you achieve one, like achieving any goal, you will be rewarded by always knowing that you can. These little wins are never going to go away. They are move along the way. Remember how to adapt your strengths to the situation to make it easier any time you move to another target. "Working intelligently not difficult" always applies wherever possible. Focus on every move until it's as comfortable as an old hat. To this day, I still sometimes ask people that I do not know for directions or help, to speak to them!! The stuff we do is tradition.

Have you ever heard the phrase "fake until you make it?" The idea behind it is simple and helps build confidence. You will start to integrate these things into your life so that they are the norm, by doing enough and putting yourself there. They're getting fast. You start to describe yourself. You are, to a significant degree, what you do. When you truly understand this concept, you begin to see that you can become anything you want to be. You take action and start defining yourself. You are looking for information right now that tells me whether you know or not; you are already following this idea. You take action to define or redefine yourself to someone more confidently. In some cases, you're learning to trust just now by taking action!

Make a commitment to yourself

Make a commitment to yourself, and you will certainly find a few stumbling blocks as you move on to your learning and begin to build self-confidence. There is always a little urge to stop, withdraw, or escape. Just note, taking the easy path is like concealing obstacles and works to undermine your trust instead of creating it. Stay dedicated to your personal growth and challenges where possible. The best thing is, even if you lose because you were standing and facing it, you will always gain confidence. You tried! There is much bravery to face the fear or the doubt and to try. It's going to make you stronger if it doesn't kill you. If it could kill you, then rethink it by all means!

Self-confidence building relies on rational thinking.

You can find that self-confidence is always going to try and a break-in. But you're going to look for it. That time it happens, learn to recognize it for what it is. When these questions come into your mind, all you need to do is to examine the situation critically and efficiently truly. Is this possible? Should people do this kind of thing? If so, then yes, you will probably learn and do it as well. On the other hand, if you doubt something because of a rational objection, a significant challenge is also possible, and a new assessment, plan, or acceptance that this is an unlikely goal may justify the situation. If you are 50 years old and you were not in the Air Force or went to school, you could be a little out of reach to an astronaut, or perhaps the road is so daunting that the means cannot explain the final result.

For example, he was determined to go to medical school and become a doctor at a certain point in a college's life. He was an excellent student, had a Bachelor's degree already, and many of the requisite courses. He was 35, however, and there were also three children and no income. He started determined and optimistic, but gradually there began to emerge questions about this path. Careful examination told him that remaining committed and confident could get him pretty well, and friends and families could do as much as they could, but it might prove more strife than worth 4-5 years to borrow money and survive on no income before you can work once again. It could not even be safe to try to deal with this while completing one of the most academically rigorous career paths. He had no practical and viable strategy that would match his current situation. Careful consideration has shown that his motive is based heavily on money and prestige, which could be poor grounds for getting his family into trouble. These achievements finally led him to review this career path as a viable option.

The moral of this is that not all suspicions are unfounded and fear motivated, but many. Be realistic in assessing your doubts and objectives. When you learn how to trust, you will also learn how to measure your goals and fears more effectively.

I hope some of these ideas will help you prepare yourself better as you go on the path to self-confidence. Take this advice and brace yourself emotionally while you continue to learn how to be comfortable in all aspects of your life. You will be more open and willing to take every course. Get ready and start making your way to a new, more confident person.

So now, what do I do?

You now have a few ideas as to how to get the head right, but also to send you confidence level up to new heights; you will need a plan and a willingness to follow it.

THE STAGES OF PSYCHIC DEVELOPMENT

The next steps will explain how close you are to' flicking the light switch' and waking up from the' sleeping man' of George. The phases do not usually occur in any specific order, they are not stone-placed, and some of them can be encountered. Nevertheless, the following order represents the order of experience of many people on the road, and the method of growth seems to be systematically approached. Many people are going through them all; some are going through one or two. Overall, however, you should evolve in the right place.

Most stages are connected to the integration of the spiritual, emotional, and energy body as a vital component of the development process.

1. Life Crisis

This stage does not need to happen to everyone on the psychic road if they note the piercings at an early stage. But the step towards spiritual creation is often followed by a life drama. It could range from a troubled childhood to a recent divorce.

2. Enhanced consciousness

It is when you begin to see things from the corner of your eyes. It could also begin by seeing the "blob" of swirling of color energies. For others, it would be that the beginning of texts, visions, premonitions, and feeling that you go insane, or the mind plays tricks. Citizens here often ignore the pebbles and deny what their enhanced senses are trying to tell them.

3. Hypersensitivity

Being more sensitive to criticism and opinions of other people. At this point, you begin to know that you can sense the feelings of other people. Confusion and the feeling that' I am normal' prevail at this stage.

4. Check

The search begins for information that describes the unusual encounters. Often this is done quietly for fear of ridicule. There is also a strong desire to find' like-minded' people. It's at this stage that you start questioning your health! It is the no-return point. You will spend your life searching for answers to the questions of life from this point forward. There may be rest, but you're always curious. It's like a sore that you can't scratch.

5. Beware! Start standing up for yourself!

The meek immediately start to stand up for themselves and accept no-nonsense. It can be short-term because it is only the beginning. A concrete base has not been installed, but the wheels will be relocated.

6. Feeling isolated/confused

At this point, the advancement of psychology has usually found material to describe their desires and the like. Unfortunately, at this point, those often closest to the individual would like to destroy the new interest of their partner/friend because they feel threatened (but will not) by this new' hobby.' A "concerned" parent also takes the psychic aside about how they get into an illusion or are brainwashed, and how everything is Mumbo Jumbo. You're fortunate if you don't have this point!

It leads to very mental confusion. Is it wrong to keep going? What should I do? What should I do? Was I mad? Am I mad? The decision is generally to live in silence and not to share new information with your immediate peers.

7. At this point, I can't do it Feelings of vulnerability surface very well.

The psychic growth makes us move faster. They cannot work out how to speed up their progress but are disheartened by the speed with which their psychic peers move around them. Many people may feel the reverse, that they are moving too fast, afraid of the experience, and want to slow down or shut down because the pressure is daunting.

Imagine waking up to you in an unfamiliar and strange world. If you were one of the fortunate few who would have been extremely curious and like to wake up in the unknown, the unfamiliar would seem to be overwhelming before you got used to it. For many, they begin to wake up in this new world, and they try to deny themselves that they awaken in the hope that things can remain the same "comfort zone," familiar and well known. This will continue until the emerging psychic is no longer terrified and wants to accept the "new world."

We've all dreaded change at some point in our lives. The key to resolve change fears to take a moment to rapidly advance life as it will be if we stay the same. Life cannot change unless we change; it just leads to disappointment if we hope it changes. In your head, quickly move your life to how it will change once. Transition is an exciting option soon to see!

8. The senses are still sharpening.
 As they are, the growing psychic may be very sensitive to loud noises at this moment, they may find that they cannot bear the radio and voice sounds. They often want to be outside or feel a strong need in the countryside. The enhanced urge to spend time alone, or 'starring through the kitchen window.' Your body tells you that you want to meditate. During this process, a daily quiet place must be found during the day to prevent irritability.

9. Awareness that your work/circumstances are wrong for you.

It is the start of learning to see bricks!! Many people wait until they are made redundant or sacked (bouldering) before they see their job/circumstance/relationship outgrown or that their workplace or home doesn't suit their current sensibilities. It is often an appalling stage because your life is often (not always) compromise up to that point. The hard thing is the confidence to go on and on.

Going through this stage often becomes a stumbling block and slows down the growth for most people. This process is about breaking away from the choices "made for you" in your life and "what you did to satisfy others." It's about getting rid of your profession because it's good for your friends, the link you have had for convenience, or the job you have done for money.

Probably the most important element in choosing the psychic route and improving your abilities to the best of your ability. You can't be a true psychic without being honest with yourself. Those who don't genuinely fear the spiritual route for themselves sometimes. Those who are genuine welcome it with themselves!

10. Feeling abandoned

This aspect doesn't necessarily happen on the psychic road to everyone.

At this point, friends and family start leaving your life or seem to disappear. The psychic creators are no longer connected with those they have worked with for years. Your life's structures start to disintegrate. Everything you thought to be true, to which you are connected, falls apart.

How poor!! It is indeed a fantastic stage so that you can see beyond the present situation. How do you restore a house that was abandoned? No, you don't! Oh, you don't! You must first knock it down to build a new, stronger one in its place.

This stage includes seeing any illusions. We find what is real through this stage. Oh, how we say lies to ourselves! We assume that everything is good when it isn't. We convince ourselves its bad when it's all right. When everything is stripped from us, we begin to understand the universe's beauty. We develop a great understanding of what is important and how the small things in life are valued. Once this stage is complete, Trivia is Trivia. What seemed tragic does not have the same feeling as before.

Uncontrollable crying is part of this stage for no obvious reason. It is because the cells of the body start throwing away old memories and making way to see your own and the lives of others.

11. Increased capacity

The psychic senses usually develop with a very good and solid base by this time. At this point, the ability to "read" people is often quite high.

12. Detox

This stage comes early for some; it comes a bit later for others. Physical illness often has to emerge and present you (a boulder) if you neglect it. The more you neglect the need for this, the more serious the physical illness is.

It's time to cleanse your body now and, if it's not done, your mind. As the ability to channel higher energies than yours increases, the energy channel must be used. If not, as with many psychics, not very fun physical disease, it starts to happen. When you fail to detox, the result is a little like filling an exhaust pipe in a potato.

Detox means fasting for a couple of days. It has many fasts, from drinking water for a day or two, to eating brown rice for breakfast, lunch, and dinner for up to 10 days. Eat less meat and sugar. Minimize the consumption of caffeine. Take lots of fresh fruits and vegetables, clean your colon. Stay away from energy-efficient food, such as taking and microwave food. If you smoke, drink too much alcohol or rely on all forms of drugs (legal or illegal), stop or stop getting help.

Please note, the use of illegal drugs is a low energy activity, so it is not just dangerous for you but to every other person. Because it is a low energy act, you draw a low energy spirit, and can't sustain the energy with adequate vibration to channel effectively. It would be too much of a leap from low energy to high energy.

13. You want to support everyone.

This stage can sound like it's a great place to be. No, it's not. You can't help anyone, but you can offer people a "leg-up" and not a "hold up." If you try to drag a person to a place where they don't want to be, but you think it's best for them, refrain-leave them alone!! Concentrate on your "self," your "family." People are all right, and you have only the right to change yourself-just leave them alone!

But those in your life will join it for a while to be polite. Just because you have already started to find this new knowledge that the world will know, you'll have the "nut case" tag in your family or circle of friends if you aren't careful. You don't have the right to ram things down others' throats. They'll ask if they're interested. If you do ram awareness (there will be a temptation), people are prepared because, at some stage, your ideas will be suspicious about' reality is what you can see.' If / when you arrive at this stage, it is only a waste of energy. We are free to recognize and follow their opinions, as they are. You don't want to shoot down your view, so it's wrong to shoot at them or back.

At this point, the psychic development in this field will typically not be extremely confident in itself or herself. You will know when you are because you don't have to tell others how to be, and they will start to have a profound respect for your involvement in the creation of your mind. In that way, it's almost ironic.

It is a test of how true you are to yourself. Few people like to be "preached," so remember to LEAVE THEM ALONE, no matter how much you can see, they are heading in the wrong direction. Offer just advice if you ask! Stop the, as they make a mistake,' Told you so.' Finally, they'll ask you for your theoretical advice before acting (maintain it non-partisan) when you've seen the predictions a couple of times. In the meantime, focus on improving yourself.

14. At this point, you know everything.

You know everything at this moment. The psychic creation gets bored by the methods they learn. Think your group holds you back;

you don't have anything else to say. The presumption begins that they have had enough training to travel and go alone, away from their peers.

Many people lose contact at this point and are seen as unreliable, even if they are all recognized in the afternoon. As this stage becomes more advanced, the more you learn, the less you need to talk, the more intuitive you are, gradually gaining great respect for their abilities when they need to teach goes away.

15. Clearing

It is the stage where the fun begins!! The clearing stage is when everything you've never done, or everything you're scared of begins to take your head. Your worst fears turn into reality, and all your insecurities are beating at you. The more you overlooked them in practice, the more pronounced they will be for clearing by the Universe. The way forward is to take up and welcome the clearing stage, for that is what will change your life for the better forever!

Generally, this stage involves a lot of crying and intense emotion. It's often best to stay with your current job and circumstances during this period. You will shake the very foundations of what you thought was safe. At this stage, psychic developments often believe that they need to change the external ones (job, relationship, etc.). It is not the case since the root of your misfortune delays the cycle. Keep the feelings you experience' processing', then change the external ones if your feelings are still the same.

Depending on psychic development, this process may last some time and occurs in conjunction with certain other steps. Through this process, the psychic development will understand that it is not a solitary process and will return to its peers for help and advice in their development group.

16. Breakthrough,

The psychic becomes extremely perceptive after the clearance (which can take a while). You can see what's going on in a hundred paces for someone because anything that opened up to a real state of being was removed during the clearing process. There's nothing that stops you then!!

The clarification stage is also necessary for the psychic's humiliation. The mineral of the great Universal force humiliates the psychic as the awakening cycle swings. A profound appreciation of all life occurs at this stage.

You start to look younger, the mind becomes very quiet, and the body is healthier so that you can manifest what you want in your life quicker and faster.

Many people think they're happy whether they earn lots of money or win the lottery. You should feel wealthy in the true sense of the word to this level.

17. Power

The most valued factor is power. Most reach the' high stakes' at this stage, and they are very good at their job-powerfully intuitive.

It is the stage when people are looking for your help. It's a real challenge. It is when the psychic abilities of a person become so amplified, they have to be very specific how they are channeled. It is why spiritual growth while on the psychic path is so necessary.

It is at this point that a psychic can transmit energies that are powerful in helping people but can also be used to power others. The real psychic must do his/her best never to exercise power over others. To do this, you will sacrifice your commitment to what people do with their lives. It is not the position of the psychic to judge other persons or guide a person's life; you are there to channel the highest possible source of information so that a person can make an informed determination about how they live.

The obtained knowledge will only be at the same level as the psychic. A highly developed guide will not move through an information medium. Like a solicitor, a five-year-old won't discuss the technicalities of the rule.

When life changes radically in the main stages of the spiritual route, all start to fall into place happily. Few things bother you, there are short-term worries, and life challenges are brief. The deprivation mentality with which most of us are afflicted starts to disappear, and we know that there is enough for all. Negative thoughts and feelings about others, and we vanish, and others get automatically supported.

Life is becoming very fast; change is constant, easy, and welcome. There is a need for a deeper understanding and knowledge of how life works. The' reading' of others becomes very straightforward with the opportunity to' upload' into and from the energies of those living and those who have gone through it with ease and little effort, using a mental adjustment. You will become the receiver, like tuning into a radio station and can turn on and off whenever you want.

The desire to live comfortably grows, but the interest in material things declines. The development of your own and the prosperity of others (in all areas of life) is the cause of celebration. Jealous words and deeds belong to the past. It is fun to accept people as good as they are. So, to satisfy you, people don't have to adjust. They are acceptable because you accept yourself.

However, this makes it easy to choose who you want and who you want to let go of in your life. Security exists at this point. The psychic discovers that by letting go, not trying to hold tight, the true progress of oneself and others could be accomplished. This point likely lost anything the psychic held tightly. It can take the form of material objects, members of the family, friends, or partners. It is so that the medium can learn to allow all energies to be free and not to be punished by their physical manifestations. Issues become an' important process of evolution' rather than a question or horrible occurrence.

Then comes sharing and enclosure—a spiritual cycle that remains unmistakable and individually private. The friendship with the Universal Force (or God if you will) achieves completeness.

It doesn't mean it's the end from this point on. The psychic draws on what has already been experienced, following the idea that life is the same but different. It's remarkable because skydiving is as fun as toilet cleaning. You may have heard the saying, "Water bears water before lighting chop wood-water holds water after clearing chop wood." Life in the outside world may not have improved, but life in the inner world is much more pleasurable.

When you find that you are not reaching all the stages as a spiritual creation, it doesn't mean you have failed. The experience of every person is different. For some, part of their life's objective is the completion of the whole spiritual journey; for others, it is meant to experience a couple of things. Life is about living; no one is more important than another. No matter what your personal journey experience is, it is 100% right for you at this stage of your life. The very fact that you find it means your trip is fantastic.

CHAPTER SIX

RELATIONSHIP THERAPY AND ATTACHMENT STYLE: THE BASICS

THE CONNECTION

It might be the kind of thing "If it were a serpent, it would bite you," but all relationships involve the nature of the relationship. When you fall in love, brain chemicals (neurotransmitter) overpower your neurology, which make you feel passion, joy, and happiness. Every one of you feels like you have met your wife, and you can only see her beauty, and you are again a very good person! The mixture is perfect when both the brains flood in excessive neurotransmitters. The brain chemicals return to normal over time, but if you have a strong connection, you begin the process between "fallen in love" and "standing in love." This period is all about the survival and sense of security of the "connection." In psychological terms, we are all linked in styles or, more specifically, an "attachment style."

The first category is Safe. It means that these people expect their partners to be there and attentive and caring for their needs. You should pray for love and love if you need it. During their times of need, they are also compassionate and open to their partners. You trust that things will work through. We easily share their feelings and accept our partners ' feelings with curiosity and reverence.

Concerned people appear to be worried that the connection is at best weak. We are distressed mentally and physiologically when there is a real or perceived danger to the relationship (i.e., when their partner said we didn't call, their partner did not care about them rather than work). You may not be sure that you can share your needs, as you do not expect to be taken care of and addressed. This uncertainty about the connection leads to actions that can alienate partners and thus build the insecurity in which they are concerned. Such habits often encourage the partner to isolate himself, aggravating his anxiety.

Avoidants also feel insecure but show their insecurity differently. When they are worried that the demands of a partnership are beyond their ability, they remove their sense of need for the connection and turn it mentally away. These are the people who say they need "space." We need space, but too often, we dial their sense of love and enjoyment of the partner by dwelling on their flaws in this room. By removing the relation, they seem calm and unimpacted, but physiological tests often suggest they are in pain, like the ones in the anxious group. When they break up with a partner, they are the people who remember how he really was a very good partner and may even lament the end of this partnership. They feel lonely again and want to be in a relationship. You can most probably see the challenges facing a concerned person and an avoiding person. One pursues the other distances anxiously. It is a frequent dynamic that can lead to frustration if it is not successfully understood and managed.

The Fearful Avoidant usually survives the trauma of some kind. They tend to want relationships but, at the same time, are quite afraid of them because people have been nursing and abusive in their past. They are more responsive to disruptions, real or imagined, and can protest dramatically. They can alternate between withdrawal and anxiety.

YOUR ATTACHMENT STYLE

We have studied the complex Attachment Styles literature very easily. Your attachment style and your partner's attachment style will greatly influence how you communicate. Most importantly, your types will warn you at the emotional level of how comfortable or insecure you feel with the ups and downs of life and relationships (no matter what you say to yourself intellectually). In and out of loving relationships. There are times when passion and connection fluctuate. There are periods when affection and connection are through. Conflicts are also emerging. Two secure people accept this ebb and flow and walk-in confrontation. You recognize that love continues, even in periods of frustration, conflict, or temporary separation (i.e., demands for work or childhood). Suspicious, preventative, and frightening people are struggling with this, and their interactions often become "protest" about their experience of a connecting threat: too little, too much, too unpredictable.

Here's the point: regardless of the war or claim, I found that the bottom line is about communication. The following section also describes how this bottom line is often overlooked in changing trends. By the way, the dating pool is weighted heavily by anxious people. The safe people prefer to wade out together from the dating pool.

THE MATERIAL TRAP

It's sometimes difficult to differentiate between "material" and "method," which sounds like a word therapist, but which is meaningless. The "material" is a topic, a problem, or a subject. "The method" is the path, the way, the means — the way. The material is something like a movie to enjoy like Les Miserables, Batman. The method is how you communicate with your partner about the film you want to see. ("You've been selecting the movie every time! It's my turn now." or "See before we find one we both like."). The cycle often becomes a pattern that is both difficult to identify and difficult to change.

Couples are often treated in the content trap. We dispute: who did what? Who said what? Basically fighting against the content. We miss the point that the very act of fighting is the problem, and they also lack the point that, in the end, the relationship, typically, is the real problem. Even if people have differences, you can communicate, but you can easily feel disconnected if you concentrate on the material (instead of the mechanism and the connection). When you feel disconnected, particularly for a long time, love may fade, and the relationship may be in trouble.

THE PATTERN MODIFYING

The practice of pair therapy consists of transcending' content' and modifying' pattern.' The material comes and goes, but when the method or pattern is working, it can be dealt with effectively, and the relationship is a good pattern. The first move is to see the "information trap" and the next "negative trap" as your enemy and not your friend. Your enemy's not your friend! The enemy is the material trap and the negative loops that follow. It's so necessary.

It's an easy one! Take a while and think about how good it is and how you feel when you're the user or manufacturer of a supplement. You love things about your friends, and they love things about you. You can build a better relationship if you can consciously concentrate on those issues and, more importantly, align your partner with what you consider. Statement starting with "I truly appreciate..." or "thank you for..." or "You are always so good at..." are perfect ways to add to the ratio of "5." It is part of the secure connection that leads to it. A feeling we get while we and our partners have challenges and mistakes, the overall experience is good and should be good for the future.

EMOTIONAL FOCUSED COUPLE THERAPY

Define the problem differently.

Our forms of attachment, luggage, the experience of relationships. Too often, our more disturbing feelings under the surface get in the way, and we are in negative relationship loops. What we need to do is understand the process and the emotions that come and go; lean back to our partner instead of turning away from him/her in fear and hurt. But it's too frightening in the cycle. And there's a good reason for this fear: it tells you to protect yourself against harm. Yet, given the best information in our minds, the things we do in response to fear, particularly in our relationships, can be counterproductive.

Nevertheless, even our counterproductive behaviors, when we understand them in the context of a threatened connection to our partner, do not make sense-either our partners or we cannot see it in the middle of the cycle. If the emotions generated are not effectively treated, attack and defensiveness or avoidance and stonewalling start, and the resulting negative process causes relationships to disappear and affection to vanish. Such depressive loops are the problem, not our partner and not our emotions. It's so necessary, if these negative cycles of relationships emerge, we often need help to change them. The most powerful way is to deal with the feelings of every person, but differently from what is normally known. If that was convenient, we would do it by ourselves. It's not easy, and it's not important for us to do it alone.

EFT

Unlike other forms of couple therapy, EFT pays close attention to the feelings that have both partners around their love and relationships (seeing all the gestures that have been made in the relationship dance from an attachment perspective. In EFT, we evaluate each person's experience and see how human history, as well as current (cycle) experiences, lead to emotions such as insecurity, anxiety, isolation, and insufficiency. Too often, in the cyclical conversations we have with our friends, these most fragile (primary) relational interactions are overlooked. We share emotions such as anger, guilt, and aggression (secondary emotions). All we see when this happens is frustration, criticism, or withdrawal. Then we write stories to explain what we see — negative stories about us, our partner, and the relationship. It is this loop (and its stories) that paralyzes the loving relationship and disables associates with warmth and love. Without support, the reality that anxiety, loneliness, inadequacy, and uncertainty are all about the lack of closeness and attachment that used to exist is easy to lose.

There is only help

When we understand that this is an important beginning, but it is only the first step. A few in trouble need help to truly understand this negative cycle, this spiraling cascade of secondary emotions and reactive behavior. Once, you need support to see that your cycle is not your companion, but a problem. You then need support to reach these more insecure feelings underneath all this and speak about the underlying emotions at play with each other. First, once you recall your need for close relationships (and it's often forgotten for a long time), the greatest risk is to reach out directly to your partner from this most vulnerable place of yearning for reconnection and understanding.

Now the couple is entering a powerful moment of reconnection, and it is hard to trust in the beginning as much as it is desired! This fresh, more insecure appeal for a revived bond appears to be ignored because it is so foreign, it goes against the stories used to make sense of the relationship so far. By listening to and taking into account the nature of a different pattern of activity, the process is often more condensed. With the aid of EFT, however, new patterns of contacts begin to emerge, and both partners begin to feel noticed, recognized and valued. Then new stories appear to replace the stories mentioned above. The perspective of the relationship changes, becoming closer to each other. It's another dance; it's a different connection. It feels very different, and this is what we have always been doing! Referring to Einstein's statement, 'Not only is information obtained but understanding based on experience.'

Another way of thinking about the relationship is in EFT that the counseling consumer is the relationship, not the people in the relationship. In the EFT, the therapist takes care of relationship patterns, feelings, stages, and dance. The EFT therapist helps all partners to strengthen their engagement, learn new steps, and gestures to this partnership. Ultimately, as a therapist, I want to help you have a more successful relationship and to respond to your needs in a way that will continue. Instead, whatever life brings you and your partner, your partnership will support and inspire you. It is what EFT does concerning relationships. Across one and 2-year follow-up studies, work has shown strong increases across relationship satisfaction even at 10-12 EFT sessions. Even with couples with chronically ill children, this is true for one of the' risk' pair styles of therapists in their offices. EFT provides a clear and comprehensible roadmap to outstanding relationship disputes and restored bonds.

EMOTION IS EMOTION - IT IS NEUTRAL

Your thoughts make it positive or negative at that moment. Emotion is an extraordinary and very mysterious phenomenon. Everyone has them, from time to time, feels up and down, and still can't understand what is behind the emotion. Emotion is a strange thing other than the saying,' a feeling that affects my mood,' that is indefinable'. Many times, in a given moment, you can experience an emotion that is not normal, and that can be confusing. Perhaps emotions come without any cause, you know. To search for a better understanding of our reality and our future, we must discuss the human and spiritual aspects of emotions. Water is water, no flavor. When placing the flavor may be coca-cola or tea, sweet or sour, minerals, sugar, or salt may be added, the taste depends entirely on what is placed in the water, but the water itself is still tasteless. Your moods will change based on events that trigger ideas during the identification process.

Emotions themselves are neutral, and your feelings direct your emotions, then you term them a positive or negative emotion depending on the mindset with which you channel emotional energies. It's not emotion, but positive or negative thoughts, that drive your emotion down this path. So you feel something and call it such an emotion. Water is simple, and you add sugar or salt by selecting what you want to taste, sweet or salty, depending on your feelings. But if you're not careful, if you're not awake and active, you might confuse sugar with salt. You want sugar, but you don't pay attention to your feelings, and you get salty. Emotions are the same, you feel, then let your mind enter a particular thought, and that thought defines your emotion, even if it's not what you feel at this moment. It is the secret to managing your emotions.

Understand what emotion is, at its heart, its neutrality and how it gets infused with positive, negative, or even neutralized, and transformed into a completely non-feeling emotion. You may have caused an emotional response and then reason it to mean nothing intellectually. The emotion is still in you, but you don't feel it because your thoughts have determined it is nothing, and it shouldn't be. If you do, the rage stays in you like a can of soda trembling and ready to explode. If another stronger emotional event occurs, it will open, and you will undergo a big explosion. If the case is a negative incident, often the most common cause as we can lose our composure and rage more quickly than we can for a positive one for a negative event, a pending emotion will come out of frustration. The pent-up emotion doesn't have to be a negative event.

It could be a heartbreak, a loved one's death, a business failure, unexpressed love or fear, something indoors without the release of the emotion, telling yourself that it was just nothing, and you're coping with it. For a negative event, it is more likely to lose your temper because anxiety is a greater motivator in instant reactions than love. It is very rational and clear. If you face the imminent danger of death, your instincts must get your body moving quickly to save you. It is done by producing adrenaline that produces an emotional effect of enjoyment together with increased physical energy. When you face love or enjoyment, you do not have to leap and respond, but you will feel and taste it in a relaxed way.

Impulses cause emotions, so strongly linked that they are almost the same. Pleasure, sorrow avoidance, the instinct of survival, hunger, fear of attack, happiness, sex, partner, species propagation, etc., all these are instincts, and they cause the emotions that we name. I'm sure you have witnessed yourself or saw someone else react negatively to something to find out that you were wrong and that the incident was a good one. When the confusion is understood, the feeling turns from negative to positive.

It shows that feelings are subjective, and only our thoughts determine whether they are considered to be positive or negative. The perception and, of course, the outcome, based on your reaction, is decided by emotion combined with thought. Perhaps emotions are much more than mere feelings. Let us now consider a much greater and deeper explanation for emotions, more metaphysical. If emotion is energy, such as fire, and thoughts will decide how this energy is used to burn the house or cook your food, could there be a "greater" reason why people have emotions? If feelings are energy, an energy that can lead us either to protect and preserve ourselves can also be used to our own needs and goals in a higher sense.

If emotions are guided and experienced based on feelings and thoughts, come both from one's mind and memories, and from experiences from outside, then perhaps emotions have a greater purpose than we do. Intuitions are ideas that come from outside of your head and then think your own. Thoughts direct emotions and decide what you're going to feel. The best way to get someone to act is via their emotions. In conjunction with these views, and with a belief in a God or a higher being or divine world with angels and celestial guides, it could be very likely that emotions have a much more powerful purpose in their creation like the human being, not only the body but also the spiritual and emotional organs. As all the tools can be manipulated or neglected, so can our minds and our mental and spiritual bodies. Let us believe that the organ of emotion was created and incorporated into the design and development of the human being.

The organ was designed to enable a human being to act and to feel. It helped to give positive energy, including compassion, affection, and self-preservation through the sense of fear and thus preventing risk. Through time and for whatever reasons that might at this time only distract us if we were to find out what they are, we have taken the direct intuition capacity away and replaced it with an intellectual thinking process. Thoughts are nostalgic. As you know, memory is skewed by simple tests to equate two people's interpretations of the same incident. Emotion is neutral in itself but intended as a motivational energy power based on directions and information received at times. Intuition is a way of receiving messages from outside your personal experience, basically a means of interacting with higher wisdom and knowledge if you prefer it to the actual word of God or even the spiritual realms. Emotion turns into thinking as opposed to intelligence.

Intellect can only receive the information it has received and worked with instead of creating emotionally out of nothing. The work of the great artist, composer, the inventor, is all focused on their emotional center. A great sculptor would say that he sees in the stone the finished product. Let us be frank now, how many of us could see "King" in a stone block. The intellect has taken over as the principal position in our lives. Intellect also took the emotional course, and from there, it was downhill. Since then, emotions are out of control and make us feel and do things we know to be harmful to ourselves and others, and have created all sorts of havoc and wars, both global and family. If we can return to the understanding that emotions are good, that thought determines the emotional feeling, and that intuition is a guide for emotional development, you can begin to regulate your malfunctions, feel emotion, find positive thinking, and get rid of negative emotions forever. It is the process of achieving any goal if you feel it is perhaps too complicated to live. If you have a target, you probably have a clear picture of your aim.

The idea is that if you feel any emotion at all, you will know that you will think about your target at that moment. Do not be afraid that your emotions are negative because when you think of your goal, your emotions will turn to your thoughts, which will be your goal. It may take a lot of time for you to do this quickly. You fight a muscle that has worked so long in one way, and now you try to change is a common practice. Nonetheless, it can certainly be done and done relatively quickly. Let us now send you some exercises to support you.

Exercise 1

Get a sugar bowl and a salt bowl with the same size, perfect or match. Mix the bowls, have someone push them like a shell game, so you don't know which bowl. Close your eyes, and try to touch one or the other. Make your choice and then check to see whether you are correct. Continue to practice as often as you can until you have the right bowl to respond to your desired option.

Exercise 2

You should note how you think of what you feel mentally, preferably negative. Of course, it takes some mental effort, but it's not that hard to do. When you realize that you are thinking about something, you feel negatively emotional, make every effort to think about something positive, your objective, or somebody you love. Maintain the feeling alive. It's not to stop or change the feeling, and it's just to change the mind.

You may have anything that activates or encourages your mind to concentrate on the positive, or you might have a photograph. If you can hold your emotion on fire and kill it, you can generate a burning desire, intense focus, and enthusiasm for your goal, and it is good. This emotional rocket fuel is what is needed to achieve any goal, and this approach creates a new habit where you feel positive when you do.

CHAPTER SEVEN

LETTING GO OF EMOTIONAL BAGGAGE

Emotions. We've all got them. Some of us are only more successful in dealing with them than others. So they stick around when we don't deal with them.

Many of us have created some emotional baggage. Past experiences produced emotional responses, and these old feelings still can be used to torment us and affect our lives today.

Emotions don't just come from the sea, although they might feel that way. A thought is behind every emotion. A negative emotion, therefore, is only a symptom of negative thinking. We think we're badly treated and upset. We assume we could fail, and we're afraid, but few take the time to recognize the feelings that produce emotions. You can even fault yourself for feeling or blame others for producing the emotion, but do not make any real attempt at discovering the root cause of the emotion.

The emphasis is often on how to "treat" the emotion. Many people use alcohol, narcotics, overeating, and other addictive behavior. Others may use emotional support groups, relaxation techniques, or exercise. However, regardless of whether we use a positive or a negative emotional approach, we deal only with the symptoms and not with the cause. The thought behind the emotion is ignored by trying to block or fight the emotion.

To let the emotional baggage go, we need to change the reasoning behind these feelings. We must, therefore, change our attention and begin first by defining the cause for the emotion. What theories make us feel the way we do? What do we do to motivate and maintain this idea? Our thoughts are based on our beliefs, so we have to determine whether we truly believe the thought we have. If not, we can choose to substitute a more positive thought for this negative thought.

Shakespeare said, "Nothing is good or bad, but thinking is." So, our emotions are just a response to the stories we tell. Such stories are the meanings we offer of events. Our thoughts on events overlay these interpretations, and the reflections on things can be real or not. Therefore, we respond to a life only contained in our minds.

Let go of anxiety and anxiety. Anxiety and anxiety are feelings frequently triggered by our inability to foresee the future. There are so many things going on in life that are beyond our influence that we can't even see what is happening.

To start reducing fear and worry, we need to shift focus, and instead of worrying about what could happen, we should think about how to plan to do whatever happens. We should concentrate on what we want the experience to offer. We can concentrate on how we want to interact. Changing our minds to reflect on our goals and priorities and making decisions on those priorities will free us from the pressure of anxiety (instead of what we think will happen or what we want to happen).

Let the frustration go. Many of us have very rigid ideas on how life should be. However, things don't always work the way we want them. We tend to run into the nature of the world and are disappointed. We can even create a "crisis" because we cannot get our way.

We should shift our thoughts about what we want from life to begin to relieve the stresses we experience. Drop your addiction to the effects of what you do and focus on what you bring into your life — using kids as an example. Children often get angry or frustrated when things don't go their way, but they generally get over it quickly and try to do something else again.

Let go of anger or rancor. Anger or distrust of others may be triggered by the belief that others "should" do things as we would like them to. The desire to control others and the views on how to behave may produce such negative emotions. We need to change our views on the actions of others, and we should alter our emotions. Eliminate the "should(s)" and focus on how we communicate.

We can feel resentment and anger towards ourselves, too. The belief that we should be perfect or that we should all know can cause us to have a negative feeling when we make a mistake or fail. Again, it may release these emotions if our perceptions and thoughts about errors shift. A mistake or error can be called a learning experience and not a disaster.

Letting go of the mindset of the victim. Blaming others for what happens to us can create a sense of victimhood or rather than considering that it's our reaction, our thoughts about the event which causes the feeling we can blame a situation. Instead of blaming others, we must take responsibility for our lives and how we react. Shift thoughts to remember your position and what you have learned or gained from your experience.

Let the frustration go. Deception can be the consequence of the feeling that we don't measure up, that we're not good enough. To scale the good ladder, whether in the company or our social life, means trying to get better or be the best. We are trying to put more money, power, or prestige into our lives to reassure ourselves or others that we are adequate. We need to redefine our views on what success means to release these feelings and let go of the need to be the best.

To achieve emotional liberty. Who stops us from being free of emotions? We do. They do. There is pain and suffering when our perceptions are not real. We have to challenge our questions about what is real for us. The truth will open and heal emotional wounds. We must analyze and alter the thoughts that cause the pain.

It is also important to feel and let go of our emotions. Again, our role models can be babies. You will notice that children are not afraid to express their feelings, but then move to other sensations very quickly. They need to know how they feel and fully experience the emotions. Recognize painful emotions and believe in positive emotions. Then follow, pass these sentiments. Emotions that are repressed will come back to haunt us later so that the emotions we have about a certain incident or question are a combination of our past thoughts and sentiments. We need to be able to express our emotions in the right way for true emotional health at the right time.

TO IMPROVE MEANS TO MAKE CHANGES! YOUR LIFE LESSONS!

Why are people changing?

Pain: You suffer from small and large mistakes which cause pain. Your lesson is to learn from your experience.

Small errors: The pain you feel over time will damage your health. Small errors don't bother you much, but big ones can have a profound effect on your pocketbook and psyche.

When you make a mistake when you turn or get off at the wrong exit on the turnstile, you can lose time if you have a big deal. That experience encourages you to leave the next time you go to an odd place. You will, therefore, use your Global Positioning System, your reference system in the car, to prevent loss and to arrive on time.

Great mistakes: Your life lessons can be devastating to your emotions by making big mistakes. You can be seriously shocked about your entire life and lose weight and purpose in life. If you lose your job but only have one skill, it's hard to get another job quickly. You must focus and think about the time you can educate yourself through higher education. If you have a huge amount of debt, it reminds you that you cannot generate higher income.

A big impact on your life will change your behavior. It can come from an alien who speaks to you at the center, a recent video, an incident on your way to work, or anything you can communicate within your life. Those encounters alone can make your life higher and confuse your friends, family, and acquaintances. Take heed to the lessons of your childhood.

With the right motivation, you will make changes to improve yourself. But the world in which you are now may prevent you from experiencing this shock and dramatic experience that you need to make the necessary changes to make greater progress.

You don't know who to turn or who to stop when various negative influences surround you. So, what are you doing to make a major positive leap into life and live a fulfilling life?

You will continue with changes in your life by doing the following things:

1. Know that you are the only one to fulfill your dreams. Keep out of negative people, places, and stuff. Write down and visualize your dreams in broad terms.

2. Believe in your skills. Have a deep desire to win something you think you can do.

3. Make sure you look at it from every perspective before you embark on anything you want to do. It can save you time and unnecessary headaches. You will have inspiration if you are ready. Develop the ability to see both sides like a coin.

4. Renunciation is not a choice. Never do it. Never do it. Face your challenge! Face your challenge. Fear exceeds the condition itself. Confront your fears and see how easy the

solution is. Life should be fun. Let nobody or anything deprive you of the natural gift. You will find that you are more driven and more motivated if you are satisfied.

5. Your family is your heritage. They are the ones in your life who matter. You can't substitute them. You have to protect them. Don't take work too seriously and think about your kids.

6. Make your fair share and more and take advantage of your life lessons. You're going to be well paid. The awards are unannounced and in barrels. Motivation and development of oneself may come from anywhere. Allow the turning a bad situation into a good one. Look at the positive things at home, college, greenhouse, parks, stores, etc. You can learn a lot by looking says a famous baseball player.

7. Your dreams are just yours, just hold on. Do not lose sight of them and find ways to do so. Always allow positive thoughts to come into your mind. Cancel the negative ones with them.

8. Ignore and replace negative with action positive comments. Don't let others with their comments to you take your inspiration and excitement. Stay away from those who people who resent your prosperity or achievements.

9. You're a unique person. No one is like you. You have a particular purpose. Figure out what it is and better give it. You are the key to your success. The secret to your failure is if you want to be all for all.

10. Try and try again. It doesn't matter how often you fail. So
    look at what you are doing and make the necessary changes
    with a critical eye, but go ahead no matter how beautiful it
    seems.

11. Love yourself for who you are. Respect yourself. Remember
    this every day. Align and surround with those who can give
    you insight and illumination to realize your dreams. For a
    long time, it will be your life lessons.

12. Once you add your ambition and inspiration, it's like putting
    on your workwear to make things happen.

13. Play fair while dealing with people. Be a direct shooter.
    Honestly, and integrity is essential.

14. Open your eyes and ears. You're going to learn a lot
    vicariously as you look at what someone does and how he
    does. Learn how things really ought to be and how they
    ought to be.

15. Take a proper workout. Do not do the wrong thing. Find out
    the right way to do it. Your inspiration will encourage you to
    know how you have never imagined.

16. Do not a quitter. Never be a quitter again. Choose the
    direction you're going. It's a winner, I think.

17. Listen to the small voice in you that tells you to start. Once you do that, others are going to follow. Be a leader. Be a leader. It creates opportunities.

18. Writing off your life and procrastinating is a waste of time and hinder progress in life going.

19. You have to take your life under control. Have a strong sense of self-control and discipline. Those two qualities are important to improve yourself.

20. Try to understand the opinions of other men. Listen more and speak less. Listen more. By listening, you learn more.

21. Visualize every chance your dreams have. If your dream is not in your level of motivation, it will be poor or non-existent. How good is a dryland boat if you're a fisherman?

22. You must be confident in your desire. More than anything else, you must want success. Dream this dream and believe your dreams. Belief is an important inspiration and self-improvement component.

23. In your career, have zip. Be a great achievement. Be different. Be different. Don't be with the majority. Typically, they're incorrect.

24. You're a unique and special person. You must, therefore, enjoy your life and nature. You're a special person. Your

existence isn't a statement. Make every second count the best you could be.

25. Take time to concentrate on your dreams, and let no one destroy you or pull you away from your deep passion for living.

WHAT CONTROLS YOUR CONSCIOUS POINT OF FOCUS?

Scientists are telling us that Prefrontal Cortex, which is a rather small area of the brain, is performing your' executive functions'- planning and controlling what you do with your brain and organism. It carries out these plans by directing your' conscious focus point' to open up certain stimulating sources.

Your Focus serves as plumbing in your brain's cellular map, whichever stimulus you willingly open to decide what is written into your neural maps. The more you concentrate on the same things actively and endlessly, the more vivid and lasting these new maps are. You can write and rewrite anything you want; as long as you are ready to write.

How you use your conscious attention tool may lead to serious emotional problems or can cure them. Your emphasis is generally referred to as "what you think about." We usually think it means working in our heads with strings of words.

In our minds, we perceive words as sounds that we call "visual self-talk" of course, they are not sounds, but a neural activity that produces an illusion. By translating these noises into a written word, we transform those sounds into images, and these images reflect both sounds and common social significance to others (have you ever looked at words like images and also sound with meaning attached to them?). Words are an example of our ability to' associate' various kinds of stimuli so that we do not even know that they are different types of stimuli in combination.

Words are quick-fire depictions of others, streams of these depictions flow in our consciousness, and we turn these streams into rational patterns of thought, yet we create with these patterns: image that shape sounds, that smell (or at least that of smells).

This cycle could be reversed.

When our values are related to meanings, they are linked to powerful emotional responses. We see in our minds new patterns concerning these sources of stimulus and associate them with previously learned patterns. The patterns are created because of intensity, vibration, and duration differences.

We can choose consciously to concentrate on all these issues, but we have to choose carefully because we have a small focus. Although there are several options here for stimulation, the number of stimuli we can actively pay attention to at any time is limited.

Only 4 to 11 bytes of electric information per second can work in our conscious brains. The more bytes we deal with at any given time, the harder it is to make sense or even recall our thinking. Once the incoming information rate exceeds 11 bytes per second, you respond to stress due to an abundance of information.

If/when your active attention works with full throttle, the neocortex uses a lot of glucose energy and tires faster than in other areas of your brain. The time you can focus on these bytes is minimal. Biologically, it's hard work to think.

Cut it out, your prefrontal cortex must concentrate your attention on 4 to 11 bytes while addressing the fact that the stimulation of your brain takes place at 2'000'000 (two million) bytes per second from your senses. To combat this amount of disruptive stimuli, most of which comes from your body due to brain impulses, which previously sent down hormonal responses, your PFC regulates the stimulus-resistance mechanism.

By the way, it is the same mechanism that you use to control and repress your emotional reactions. The root-like reticular formation in the brain stem is the principal stopping mechanism of this system. The Reticular Formation is designed to control the electrical/emotional energy level flowing at any time into your brain.

The Reticular Formation extends from your brain stem to the net-like Ascending Reticular Activation System (also known as ARAS-this system makes us aware of the world around us). Different parts of your reticular system will provide every electrical stimulation and channel it in different parts of your brain. There is, for instance, a layer of reticular material that covers the Thalamus, the main sensory signal router between the superior conscious brain and the lower emotional brain.

Without this integrated resistance device, you would not be able to focus on anything but a mass of sensory information. In emotional disorders, however, the resistance mechanism has been used in such an efficient way that the emotional stress in the body is overwhelmed and captured.

An emotional load trapped in the body keeps you alert, leading to an internal battle between your prefrontal cortex and two other inner systems for the control of your "thinking focus point"; your Orientation Response and your emotional alert system. When these two mechanisms are triggered, they regularly regulate your conscious focal point and it causes a constant state of physical stress in your body and creates a violent struggle between how your PFC wants you to feel and how your body tries to tell it what it feels.

When a person does not have an emotional disorder, he or she normally focuses on anything that his or her senses are at the moment. There is no internal control combat and no sense of tension.

Your orientation reaction and your emotional alert system–Your emergency management The PFC deals with long-term strategic self-management. It works with such things that change your self-image; choose which kind of world you want to stay in; plan the path it takes to reach and set the reasons for keeping yourself healthy throughout the journey.

In comparison, the orientation response and emotional alert are emergency solvers designed to handle unforeseen life events. One is an automatic process designed to scan for and identify potential threats, while the other aims to make the body function as a matter of urgency, by approaching threats from the highest source of energy.

Is it a Spider? No, it is a bit of fluff. It is the mechanism that suddenly pulls our attention away from what we are currently making, to pay attention to something different than we have recently become vaguely aware of.

From the corner of your eye, you can see a small fluffy blob on the surface, and see if it's a spider. It's a little fluffy. You go to take a bath and see the white enamel in black. You can't refuse to look. It's an apple grain. How did that get there? Who eats apples in the bathroom?

Your perceptive distortion partially preprograms your response to orientation. Your perceptual partiality is your implicit list of things that you want to avoid. If you go to the toilet, you are pre-programmed to see what should not be in the bathroom now.

Once you leave the shower, you are now ready to learn how the apple seed has gone there.

The response is also intended to pay attention to the new, fast-moving, the small, the potentially itchy, the unknown, the large, and the scraping sound, which sounds like it's at home. The only way to satisfy this response is to pay attention actively to the source of concern before you look at it in full, mark it as safe, and then let it go. Which completes the release process for this portion of our conscious concentration system, and you can go back to what you wanted to concentrate on previously.

If you pay attention to unknown and unexplored stimuli in sufficient detail and time to the degree that it is considered secure by your unconscious systems, they will continue to take care of your conscious concentration.

You've been waiting for that bit of fluff; I know you did.

If you've got an addiction and you don't understand how obsessions work, and you're not sure about dealing with these things so much that you cannot simply put them together without your deliberate attention against your will, it's the orientation process that continues to cause this to occur. The other explanation is that you have a high emotional signal in your body.

Your Emotional Warning System Emotional response is activated by a real-life event or imagined event (imagined so effectively that your Unconscious emotional system believes that it's real). The emotional response travels through the body to the brain to solve the problem found by the brain so that the entire body and brain take appropriate external action for the alleged problem.

The trouble is when your brain says' no' to the emotional answer, and your PFC reverses the energetic response to your body. The answer, therefore, remains in place, the body remains active, waiting for' go' from the brain. And it's waiting, but not long. It remembers the brain by coming up again through the body and trying to connect with the question in the brain, and again, the brain says' not yet.'

Your body is in a state of continuous emotional pre-release, and the emotional response, which remains for a lengthy period, continues to pursue release through a process known as projection and keeps tampering your brain to pay any attention to it. Now it comes up with stimuli that are even somewhat similar to the original question. Sadly, the brain has now forgotten what the original problem was and refuses to recognize that the response must be released.

Who, then, are you?'.

The PFC refuses to leave the body emotionally, declaring' things are wrong with my emotional system' when the reaction fails to appear.

You still re-trigger your orientation reaction because you have no idea what the repeated images are, and the emotional charge that tries to leave the body through the usual release process re-stimulates your brain.

Want to turn off your fascination with the Emotional Alert?

To eradicate an addiction or any other emotional issue, the emotional warning must be turned off. There's nothing you can do about your reaction to the orientation, but once you dig into your fascination and the emotional response attached to it, and know what there only "fluff is" it starts calling for your Conscious Attention.

Your PFC is grappling with the reality of how your emotional system works by creating systems that bring your lower brain components into resistance. To stop the struggle inside, it must change its strategy and decide to take your Conscious Focus in the emotional environment directly, and it spent so long struggling.

Through consistently surrendering to its rival competitors ' demands for control of your consciousness, it will gradually release the emotional reaction behind the emotional warning state and return to its position as normal and comfortable control of your conscious concentration.

THE MYSTERY OF LIFE'S PURPOSE

At a point in the life of each person on Earth, they will undoubtedly and eventually come together to question their purpose for existence. The foundation of this deep question often starts with the ideas centered on the reason I am here, and my focus appears to be a journey experiential via that mystery that we call life.

Many of us have encountered these seemingly strange moments in which we find the solutions to solidify our lives and believe that we're not constructing our lives on sand. Even if these moments in life allow a conscious awakening that requires our attention, they are often masked or enclosed as momentous events throughout our lives.

It is not always so because many seemingly mundane moments of life are the seed of questions but still unanswered and if we look closely, the deep answers in those special moments are lovingly contained. This has laid bare the idea that the world and everything within it is continuously created by cycles from the same fountain of life, it surely makes logical sense to believe that natural laws of life rule our nature and can very well provide solace in a tumultuous sea of questions of life. It is thanks to the proper knowledge and application of these "laws of life" that we can live fully in the moment in which we appreciate the journey of life, where we are, at any given time, in the Now of life. However, we still live in a delicate world that requires us to plan for a future while we co-exist.

Could these well defined universal Laws of life help us to understand the mysteries of life better while providing a strong foundation on which to receive guidance and answers? Briefly, the answer is yes! By applying the level of understanding, and depending on these laws of continuous precision, we will soon be aligned with powerful forces to raise our lives to the level of happiness.

If we could agree that all possibility exists in the present moment and remain centered in the Now of life, allowing the rules of life freely to work through us, we will soon recognize which we are in a co-created world that we individually have a responsibility to bring to reality. Through these simple laws, we build new Earth as we receptively accept our ultimate purpose for life itself. We are strong co-creators, and life is also our school and playground.

Laws of Life

There are many laws of life, but in this position, we will focus on only four important master laws that give birth to everyone else. Since all life in the universe of creation lies within the boundaries laid down by certain laws, we know and understand some of these. There are four fundamental, universal laws of utmost value, and they are the ones to be addressed.

It will decide our experiences through our comprehension and application of the wisdom of these four laws of life that we will appreciate throughout our lives. In our lives, many of our questions arise from the realization that the decisions we made have produced the very contrasts. Some of these experiences are unique, while all on Earth can share others.

Our collective (or individual) reaction to the events that generate our life experience is needed to enable us to challenge what we want to encounter using a comparison between different experiences. Combine the cyclic movement of life with how we understand it—the Law of Love, the Law of gratitude, the Law of cause and effect, and the Law of attraction—many questions about life are well-balanced, and answers that were once out of reach becomes vividly apparent.

It would be good to know before we come into each Law that these laws are unchangeable and that one cannot "break" them here during life, as we work in the freewill parameters. By choice, you can turn consciously or unconsciously against one of these basic laws of life, and your life experience would reveal that something was "miss" mainly out of balance. If your life course was not adjusted through the interrogation/response process we all undertake, your experiences would be further amplified while the essence of your life experience remains the same.

We all heard the question put to you like this:' Why does this always happen to me?' Read on to find out the nature of these four laws of life and how to acknowledge their signatures in your lives. When we get a more thorough understanding of how all aspects of our lives permeate them, we are motivated internally to co-create our own lives and, indeed, our universe at the same time through the unlimited power that these laws of life have.

The Theory of Love

"God is Love" is often said and conceptualized. The definition of this term is now very low in the context of the humanities and rightly so. The human expression of this first rule of life–the Law of Love–can be incredibly difficult to express in such a way that it promotes a true flow of all that embraces force. Human expression of Love is usually limited and conditional in the worst case. I'm not trying to convey human Love in all its beauty and weaknesses, but the first source of the Law of Love that empowers us to express Love in a filtered and human perspective.

While we may think that Love is a byproduct created by an external influence, we embody the Law of Love by allowing Unconditional Love to flow through us forever. This strong Law is never withdrawn from our control, just because it does not seem lost. It is only through this understanding or recognition of this unlimited source of Unconditional love that our human expression of Love originates.

Like all laws, unconditional Love

It is pure energy and is present all across the universe from the greatest to the least of creation. The Law of Love is the building block that unites all of creation, and we can either permit or deny that creation is active in our lives. Once you allow the Law of Love to rule your actions, you have become unconnected with forced outcomes which have released your will. The Law of Love brings us all together through the union of opposites to one another, and, if we apply this reality, it is the false human condition to see things as different from us that opens our hearts to allow the Law of Love to operate freely.

By practicing an open heart, especially in circumstances that seem unable to resolve, they are suddenly transformed by the Law of Love. The Law of Love teaches us that we cannot experience complete joy while maintaining resistance by not accepting our experiences. Letting go allows the Law of Life to flow and provides answers to those hard questions of life. The Law of Love-its magic part and energy science part.

The Law of Gratitude

The Law of Gratitude like the Law of Love, the Law of Gratitude, exists as a byproduct of having an open heart. This rule is the secret to your life's greater well-being and prosperity. One big reason for the Law of thanksgiving to flow in your life is because it encourages the release of endorphins chemicals in the body that impact every cell and encourage feelings of hope, relaxation, and satisfaction. Through releasing endorphins, cortisol, and norepinephrine, stress hormones concurrently decrease rapidly.

That alone might be enough reason to apply the rule of thanksgiving daily; feel great and get healthier! The acknowledgment that you are an important part of expressing gratitude brings more riches and also have respect for yourself and appreciate your greatness. When you focus on your gifts and other thankfulness, you cannot help but know that negative emotions cannot be considered simultaneously.

Gratitude requires knowing comparisons because this is how the most strong and beneficial results are felt. The rule also expresses itself as an "attitude of the mind," and to a certain degree, it is valid. The Law of Gratitude is initiated from the heart, and our mind adds visuals to the energy that encourages us to be thankful if we can allow the cycle to continue. We often misinterpret the true meaning and definition of gratitude simply because we need a different or an opposite point of view to be able to recognize that for which we are grateful. Most of the people are used to finding what is missing in their lives rather than going in the reverse direction in a chest full of treasure of items deserving of respect, gratitude, and gratitude.

For example, by understanding the lack of something you like, you bring distinguishing clarity that can easily give thanks to its nature, whether physical or non-physical, regardless of the object or the location. In addition to the more common sources-the external, recognizable artifacts of praise or gratitude-thoughts will remind us of the Law of gratitude.

Using a conscious and deliberate everyday practice of the Law of Gratitude, we become renewed hope and gratitude for our whole life, banning control, which robs opponents of fear, indignation, and other negative emotions. Any thankfulness for what you have is rewarded with an understanding that you are grateful more and that everything you want in your life comes from the rule of thanksgiving. Your decision should be simple, let the rule of gratitude flood into your life with more joy.

The Law of Cause and Effect

It is one of the most misunderstood laws of life because of the presumption that everything is supposed to happen due to certain previous actions. From an intervention point of view, expectations of future events will come to fruition if no possible changes are made simply because the root cause has been set in motion. A belief that even if a future event changes the root causes, they cannot alter our destiny can lead to fatalism, in which you resign that everything is predestined and that change cannot be caused. It is a mistake and should be kept in mind since it has no basis for the operation of this statute.

The law of cause and effect, known in the Buddhist philosophy as karma, states that the present condition of the person represents previous life decisions, which could even include many previous lives of accumulation. It is expressed as a generational curse in Hebrew doctrine and, in some way, is related to parental DNA heritage. Regardless of doctrine, it is important to note that we have the power to overcome any possibility of predisposition by our current actions and emotional/mental state. The beauty of the Law of Cause and Effect lies in it.

One of the best ways to allow your life to flow through this strict, transformational rule is to apply the Golden Rule in your heart. Do so from a viewpoint that will not only help you directly but also the world around you. Karma or the rule of cause and effect may carry a bit of forecasting when it is neglected and, if it is violated, the time takes its toll on events, and life scales are balanced. Again, the accumulation of previous acts only stimulates the flow of this energy. This intense emotion occurs in both polarities and is expressed as what can be perceived to be positive or negative action/reactions.

The implementation of this rule is easily followed if we actively strive to give away what we want for ourselves. Regardless of whether there are physical actions or thought-forms, whatever energy we irradiate, the World reacts. Accordingly, it's because what is like itself is pulled into being. Find your thoughts and actions. Much as the Law of Gratitude works, if you wish more like happiness, friendship, good health, etc. give it away from an open heart and see the Universe react in kind.

When this law is firmly rooted in your heart, you don't have to worry about policing your thoughts as this procedure is automatic as breathing. Since most of us exist primarily in the 3rd dimensional Universe, we do not have to worry too much that the law of cause and response is immediate. Luckily, there's a delayed response for now, but when you set this rule in motion, you can find that your perception is fast jumping and its consequences often appear almost instantaneously in your life and others. When this is detected, know that you receive information from the fourth dimension.

Pay close attention to things that are now occurring on Earth to experiment with this rule at an empirical stage. Choose any category- economics, politics, geophysical changes, social changes, etc. all these evolve exponentially at an ever more repetitive pace. In many ways, these events can be linked to cyclic action using the Law of Cause and Effect. For the sake of life's guidance about the power and effect of the Law of Cause and Effect, one should agree that we are an involved, integrated participant by our will and that what we do indeed creates a ripple in the sea of life and the life of others. You become profoundly aware of the power of this rule, as you create your experience evidence because whatever you believe is your reality and it moves elements of your existence expressed and practiced by the laws of cause and effect.

The law of attraction I think that everybody who has an interest in improving oneself or who wants to find the elusive "potion" or "spell" for living life has come up against the basic idea of the law of attraction. It is no surprise that a whole industry has arisen trying to pay for the growing popularity of this subject financially. If this is what it takes to help some of us understand that each of us has the power to transform and potentially co-create the Universe, then that is a great start.

The Law of Attraction states that whatever you concentrate your focus on with a higher level of emotional energy and have no opposing opposite thinking, the energy amasses to the point that the essence of the attraction is built into your life. It could also be summarized as-What is like is drawn.

An increasing knowledge base derived from quantum theory affirms the validity of the fundamental aspects of this law. While this law is far from new because the Universe is the designer and has been in use since the creation of dawn. We see the unlimited power inherent in this law on a global scale, and I believe that it has been and is used to guide the thoughts of those who are unaware of their capacity to deliver anything that focuses their attention (as correctly applied) in an environment of their design and desire.

There is also very good evidence to suggest that a large part of the "2012 change" is due to our awakening to a scientific understanding that we are completely capable of transforming this world at the global level into one that most Earth's people would call Heaven. The wonderful point in the law of attraction is that all physical manifestations are born first of emotions, then of thinking. It makes sense because feelings are genuinely powerful. Most purely, his nature focuses deeply and profoundly on our reality.

What many don't understand when trying to apply this rule, the conscious AND unconscious thoughts play an important role in the pace at which the desired result happens. "Ask, and you will receive" The Cause and Effect Theory is not far away from the Attraction Law. Both are similar laws, as are two subconscious and conscious minds; the laws work in harmony. The imaginative force contained in this legislation can be used by the mere act of being a conscious thinker. Emotions that surround thoughts are the main indicator of what you start creating and eventually appear in your life. This emotional component is a wonderful tool that is essential to know the direction and outcome of what you invite.

There is a liability for the unethical, malicious implementation of this statute. The Universe does not judge or filter out the result. You will always obtain the meaning of your thoughts on time. And just as the immediate expression of thought processes within the law of cause and effect offers an integrated, undisputed emotional guidance system. Know how your thoughts make you feel when you focus on what you want to create. If those thoughts feel good, you comply with your hopes and intentions; if you do not feel so good, turn your thoughts into a better feeling. It raises the emotional energy in the direction of your wish.

Finally, the pace at which thoughts are physically transformed into life in our world is determined by the level of the agreement without doubts or opposite convictions and the appropriate level of mental energy. All these components have to fit and work easily in your life to have full effect.

Yes, it can be a fine balance to use the law of attraction effectively and knowingly, and our physical interaction is at present required with a higher level of active intuition to advance things in the right direction. It is never done aggressively. Yes, the true full power is all in the balance of our feelings, emotions, and passionate desires without any inner conflicts over what we want to make.

Over the years, couple therapy has undergone numerous changes. Different treatment models have appeared in the clinical arena, as well as an understanding of the psychology of relationships. In my evolution as a couple of therapists, I've read and studied various models, and I've found that Emotionally Focused Couple Therapy is not only most reminiscent of me but also of the many couples in my office that help me to see relations.

Pairing Democracy is amid a democracy. The key element of this transition is the emergence of new knowledge of love and love. As Yogi Berra told us, "When you don't know where you're going, you end up somewhere else." It is hard to know how to concentrate your decisions on identifying problems and moments in your relationship without a simple definition of love and the cycle of attachment and disconnection. It is difficult to know what improvements will make a difference and what the overall goal of couple therapy is. If love is "a poisoning mixture of sex and feeling which no one understands," as Marilyn Yalom in her book The History of the Wife suggests, pairing therapy is only suitable sitcom content. Gender and emotion seem central to love, as she says, but this must not be a complete mystery.

The new science of love relationships has many branches, but they are all brought into contact in the growing literature on adult attachment, the research on emotional ties between mothers and kids. The viewpoint of attachment provides a clear and efficient map of the distressing conflict between partners.

The multitude of research on the psychology of adults which have emerged over the past decade warns us that the nature of love is not a mutual sharing of resources (so why teach negotiation skills?), a bond, a normal way of getting you together and passing on your genes, or a fleeting episode of psychotic addiction.

Love is a unique kind of emotional bond, which millions of years of evolution have introduced to our brain. It is an obligation to love. The human brain codes loneliness and alienation as danger and the emotional reactivity of loved ones as comfort, which encourages maximum resilience, continuous learning. A lack of relations with a collection of fear-responses, in his neurobiological research. As Bowlby states, the word "anxiety" and "rage" are derived from the etymological root, where both occur at times of separation while the attachment figure does not respond. This need for emotional connection is not a sensation. The fundamental concept of who we are and what our fundamental needs are, namely that we are social animals who search for such a relation, is expressed in health studies. It is now clear, for example, that mental stress is more dangerous to your health than smoking and increases the risk of heart attack.

Attachment theory suggests that we need to have a haven relationship when life is too much for us and gives us a stable basis from which we can enter the world comfortably. It is a real dependency. Many psychotherapists learn that they are too close or undifferentiated from loved ones. The method explored here offers a broader picture. The evidence shows that safe, close connections are not weaknesses but a source of power and personality integration. Studies show that a more coherent, constructive sense of oneself is firmly linked. Eighteen months after 9/11, researchers Chris Fraley found that securely linked survivors, who could turn to others to help them emotionally, could cope with and learn from this trauma, while insecurely attached survivors had major mental issues. Secure connections are determined by mutual emotional accessibility and reactivity. This is the heart of the drama in the office of the couple therapist. The struggles that matter in a relationship is about children or money only superficially. Partners will spend many hours talking about these issues rather than focusing on how the couples speak and, in particular, the key questions about interactions that lead a couple to negative dance. "Do I matter to you?" "Can you turn to me and address me?" Friends often don't know how to pose such questions, and therapists sometimes ignore or even view them as a sign of immaterial dependency.

If you look through the attachment prism, the destructive spirals that unhappy couples build and are victims of are all about the pain of separation–the privation and emotional hunger induced by emotional disconnection. If we can't get a connection to react to us, we are wired up, first optimistic, then furious, desperate, and coercive. We are looking for touch in any way we can. My client tells me, "I poked him and poked anything from him, to know how important I was for him." If we don't have an answer, frustration and depression come and claim us. This approach allows the therapist to encourage couples to see the game in terms of the ball and to fight together against the mutual enemy of loneliness and negative dance, which dominates their relationship. It also means that other strategies such as intuition or coping skills are unlikely to be effective unless the underlying issues of attachment and primary fear are addressed.

If we are unable to find a way to turn to our partner and form a sense of secure connection, there are only two other secondary approaches available to us, and they map two emotional situations with exquisite reasoning. Strategy one is to be caught in fear of abandonment and reactivity by reproaching; unfortunately, this often scares the other person and pushes him away, particularly when the strategy is normal and automatic. Strategy 2 is to swallow attachment needs and feelings and avoid (and conflict) interaction, that is, to close and delete. Unfortunately, that shuts out the other guy. These secondary strategies are ways to try to attach oneself to a relationship of attachment and deal with hard feelings but often backfire. Across EFT research and activities, we have been able to define partner's relational experiences by using these techniques. When they can order and mark their emotions, blamers speak about their partner being alone, deserted, unimportant, lost, and meaningless. They are extremely vulnerable under their wrath. Retractors talk of being embarrassed and reluctant to learn of mistakes. You assume they can never satisfy your partner and therefore feel helpless and frozen.

Attachment-based pair therapy, in this way (with attachment-based combination therapy), couples can reconcile (or even marry!), extremely positive bonding events occur. The partners begin to look more deeply at each other and are more honest and caring. A relation allows each of them and opens the door to all the advantages that research tells us is secure. A way to deal with their feelings, their loved ones, and the world that now has a haven, is shifting. Bonds research suggests that lovers are potentially overwhelmed by cuddle hormone, oxytocin, when they bond in this way. It is triggered during orgasm, breast-feeding, or just if fasteners come close to us. Oxytocin is also linked to the release of dopamine, which is a pleasure-linked natural opiate and decreases the stress hormone cortisol. The neurochemical basis of connecting the physical origins of the tranquil euphoric feeling of love is no longer a mystery. Once a pair can create such interactions, they can move into the final phase of EFT consolidation.